W9-BXZ-435
You Want Me to Teach WHAT?
Sure-Fire Methods for Teaching Physical Science and Math

# You Want Me to Teach *WHAT?*

## *Sure-Fire Methods* for *Teaching* **Physical Science** and **Math**

**Norman LaFave**

Arlington, Virginia

Claire Reinburg, Director
Jennifer Horak, Managing Editor
Andrew Cooke, Senior Editor
Wendy Rubin, Associate Editor
Agnes Bannigan, Associate Editor
Amy America, Book Acquisitions Coordinator

**ART AND DESIGN**
Will Thomas Jr., Director
Lucio Bracamontes, Graphic Designer

**PRINTING AND PRODUCTION**
Catherine Lorrain, Director
Nguyet Tran, Assistant Production Manager

**NATIONAL SCIENCE TEACHERS ASSOCIATION**
Francis Q. Eberle, PhD, Executive Director
David Beacom, Publisher

1840 Wilson Blvd., Arlington, VA 22201
*www.nsta.org/store*
For customer service inquiries, please call 800-277-5300.


15 14 13 12     4 3 2 1

*NSTA is committed to publishing material that promotes the best in inquiry-based science education. However, conditions of actual use may vary, and the safety procedures and practices described in this book are intended to serve only as a guide. Additional precautionary measures may be required. NSTA and the authors do not warrant or represent that the procedures and practices in this book meet any safety code or standard of federal, state, or local regulations. NSTA and the authors disclaim any liability for personal injury or damage to property arising out of or relating to the use of this book, including any of the recommendations, instructions, or materials contained therein.*



**Library of Congress Cataloging-in-Publication Data**
LaFave, Norman J. (Norman Joseph), 1958-
You want me to teach what? : sure-fire methods for teaching physical science and math / by Norman LaFave.
p. cm.
Includes bibliographical references and index.
ISBN 978-1-936959-01-3 -- ISBN 978-1-936959-88-4 (ebook) 1. Physics--Study and teaching (Secondary) 2. Mathematics--Study and teaching (Secondary) 3. Effective teaching. I. Title.
QC20.8.L34 2012
510.71'2--dc23

2011046960

# CONTENTS

# CONTENTS

# PREFACE

## Why This Book and Why Should You Listen?

**SO, WHY AM** I writing this book? I am certainly not the first educator to write a tome on the nuts and bolts of teaching science and mathematics. However, with new policy requirements for schools and districts to improve their standardized test scores, increased performance pressures on teachers, and severe shortages of teachers in science and mathematics comes an urgent need for proven methods to help new or struggling science and math teachers.

The teacher shortages are especially problematic. Here are some facts (Hackwood, Dynes, and Reed 2006; Hampden-Thompson, Herring, and Kienzl 2008; Markow, Moessner, and Horowitz 2006; NCCTQ 2007):

- Teachers of mathematics and science leave the field at a significantly higher rate than teachers in other subject areas. Annual turnover for science and mathematics teachers stands at 16%, compared to 14.3% for all teachers and the 11% turnover rate for all other professions. Causes for the higher turnover rate are primarily pay and professional support, with many of the teacher losses occurring within the first six years a teacher is employed. Projections for many states demonstrate that retention of science and mathematics teachers will continue to be a problem well into the future.
- The retention problem is disproportionately more acute in high-poverty schools. Data suggest that a significantly higher number of teachers who change schools or leave the field came from schools in high-poverty communities rather than from other communities. The increase compared to all schools is more than 2% in both areas.
- Many mathematics and science teachers lack adequate preparation, and this is even more acute in schools catering to high-poverty communities. More than 20% of science teachers, more than 50% of physical science teachers, and more than 25% of mathematics teachers in high schools do not have majors or minors in the field they teach. The comparative data for middle schools are even more alarming. Approximately 40% of all science teachers, more than 80% of physical science teachers, and more than 50% of mathematics teachers lack minors or majors in

the field they teach. In addition, these numbers are 10% higher in high-poverty schools than in low-poverty schools. Projections suggest that these numbers will likely increase for the foreseeable future.

Due to these shortages, school districts often are forced to place teachers in teaching assignments well outside their comfort zones, with little initial support. Courses that had been the venue of the most experienced master teachers are now being forced on young teachers with little or no experience, often without significant coursework in the field they are asked to teach. Interviews of teachers at conferences and professional development sessions demonstrate serious concern and apprehension regarding this trend. For instance, it was enlightening to observe the number of new teachers at a recent advanced placement (AP) physics institute, fresh out of a college program, who were asked to teach AP physics, sometimes with only a biology or chemistry background. The trepidation of these young teachers during problem solving and laboratory sessions displayed the crux of the problem. Many are well aware that they have the added burden of achieving high standardized test scores to receive positive professional evaluations, which adds to their stress.

Another group of teachers entering the pool comes from industry. These teachers have little or no teaching experience outside their certification programs, and although often very knowledgeable, they feel a certain degree of inadequacy from a pedagogy standpoint. It is the lack of teaching experience, not material knowledge, that these teachers must deal with in their new occupation.

Then the act of achieving learning in the students must be considered. No teaching can be called truly effective without measurable assessment of learning by the students. Achieving this efficient dissemination of knowledge requires techniques that include everything from teaching methodologies to inspiration initiatives to effective classroom management.

So, why should you listen to me? Because I have a unique perspective on the problem due to the three stages in my own professional teaching career. My experiences have allowed me to develop a system that has proven successful in helping students learn science and mathematics more effectively from a variety of perspectives: methodology, inspiration, and classroom management. In addition, my work as a professional scientist and engineer has provided methodologies from those fields that were employed in the refinement and testing of the teaching techniques presented in this book.

My first exposure to teaching science came as a graduate student. I was assigned to teach engineering physics laboratory and then physics laboratory for education majors two years later. During this era, when I primarily taught freshmen, I gained a surprising realization of the varying capabilities of students coming out of high school in science and mathematics. I can still remember grading the first lab reports and the first physics tests for students who were at the university to become engineers. I was shocked to observe so many deficiencies in their knowledge base from subjects that these students were supposed to have mastered before entering the university.

During this time, concerned about the number of students who were falling behind in their classes, I set up tutorials on my own to try to mitigate some of these deficiencies and keep these students in school. The question I kept asking myself was, "How did these deficiencies occur in the first place?" Discussions with the students provided me with a vague idea as to the causes, but not the specific details. I had success getting some of these students back on track with their studies, but others—overwhelmed by the pace and difficulty of their studies and too far behind to catch up—fell by the wayside.

It should be noted that I considered many of these failing students to be quite intelligent, but it became obvious that they were unprepared in the area of their foundation of base knowledge and skills. Many came to college with so many deficiencies that they just could not maintain a reasonable pace. I remember one student who came to me to let me know he was dropping out of college. Here was a young man who was leaving school with thousands of dollars in student loans to pay back and no degree. I wish I could tell you this was an isolated occurrence in my experience at the university, but it was not. I must say that this wasting of talent and potential bothered me greatly and fueled my first interest in the development of teaching techniques.

Later in my life, I offered my services as a tutor to students in high school mathematics and science courses. With more direct access to these students during their actual high school experience, I began to see more of the details of the deficiencies and how to resolve them. Many of the students I tutored had deficiencies in study and organizational skills and higher-order thinking abilities. They struggled to organize their learning and work, resulting in disorganized thought processes. They lacked foundational abilities, such as the ability to memorize facts and procedures. Furthermore, they failed to see the patterns underlying the subjects they were learning, thus struggling to get a grip on a basic requirement of good problem solving.

During this time, I began the development of the first rough methods that eventually evolved into the methodologies presented in this book. My tutoring provided an excellent test-and-refine environment for developing the techniques, and I found that after some trial, error, and refinement, my students had great improvement in their grades. Still, most of this was done with small groups of students in an isolated environment. I knew that to be useful for the classroom teacher with many students, some refinements and trials would have to be done in an actual classroom environment with representative populations.

Finally, I found my way to teaching at a high school. I started my career as a chemistry teacher in an at-risk high school and now teach physics at the same school. Having a true class environment at my disposal, I began to refine the methodologies I had developed to account for the realities of the modern classroom. Methods that I had used successfully with 2–8 students had to be altered and tested with classes of 24–30 students and within the constraints of a scholastic environment. New methodologies specific to classroom teaching were developed and added to the tool set, many in the areas of classroom management and study habit development.

The tools and techniques presented in this book are not purely research-based recommendations, but a set of classroom-tested methods developed over a 20-year period. These methods have demonstrated results with a wide range of students in a variety of science and mathematics courses over several years. The methodologies cover seven areas pertaining to teaching and learning, most—but not all—specific to the mathematics and science classroom: student psychology in the classroom, mastery learning techniques, study habits and skills, concept acquisition, higher-order thinking, problem-solving methods, and analytical thinking for the laboratory. In each case, I have attempted to give a basic description with enough detail to allow the teacher to try the technique in the classroom and enough flexibility so that a teacher can customize the technique to specific classroom realities and student needs. Like all techniques, the amount of success will vary due to many factors in our complex education environment. Still, the methods have been found to work across a wide variety of lessons, students, and learning environments.

Over time, I have shared many of these techniques with colleagues who have used them successfully in their own classrooms. With a growing deficit in the number of mathematics and science teachers, many new teachers are being enlisted to teach upper-level math and science courses right out of college or certification programs, much earlier in their careers than would have been the case in the past. It is my hope that these teachers, as well as others looking to improve their success rates, will find the techniques outlined in this book useful in their classrooms and will attain the improvement and success for their students that I have found with mine.

## References

Hackwood, S., B. Dynes, and C. Reed. 2006. *Collaborating to address the math and science teacher shortage: A state-university-business partnership.* Washington, DC: Business Higher Education Forum.

Hampden-Thompson, G., W. Herring, and G. Kienzl. 2008. *Attrition of mathematics and science teachers.* Washington, DC: U.S. Government Printing Office.

Markow, D., C. Moessner, and H. Horowitz. 2006. *MetLife survey of the American teacher: Expectations and experiences.* Washington, DC: Committee for Economic Development, in partnership with the MetLife Foundation.

National Comprehensive Center for Teacher Quality (NCCTQ). 2007. *Recruiting quality teachers in mathematics, science, and special education for urban and rural schools.* Washington, DC: NCCTQ.

# ABOUT THE AUTHOR

**Dr. Norman LaFave** has spent the past 30 years as a scientist, engineer, author, and educator. He has performed science and engineering work for the U.S. Navy, U.S. Air Force, NASA, the FAA, and Lockheed Martin Corporation. In addition, he has managed an engineering consulting company, Dynamica Research, that has performed work for various companies and entities.

His work in theoretical physics has included research in space-time structure and quantum gravity. His aerospace engineering projects have included work on the Space Shuttle, International Space Station, lunar gravitational wave observatory design, the conception and design of a commercial space launcher for the X-Prize competition, and project management of the FAA's Integrated Terminal Weather System.

Interest in the education of young people and the innovation of inspirational teaching methods in science has led Dr. LaFave to a high school classroom, where he is currently involved in the development of a laboratory engineering concept to teach science and mathematics to at-risk students through creative and innovative projects in engineering.

Dr. LaFave has a bachelor of science degree in physics and mathematics from Carnegie-Mellon University and a doctorate in mathematical physics from the University of Texas at Austin. He has been awarded an Air Force Weapons Laboratory Fellowship and a National Research Council Associateship and has received awards for his work as an engineering project manager and physics instructor, including the NASA award for engineering excellence, the FAA Award for Outstanding Project Management, and the Texas Exes Award for Outstanding Teachers for 2010.

Dr. LaFave is the author of more than 20 professional publications in physics and aerospace engineering and recently released his first science fiction novel, *Nanomagica*.

Dr. LaFave has been married for 27 years to his wife, Shannon, and has two children, Jillian and Brock. He has a keen interest in the arts, literature, sports, and public policy. He resides in Houston, Texas.

# CHAPTER 1
## Inside the Teenage Noggin

### The Research Findings

A teacher's success in instructing teenagers is substantially enhanced the more the teacher understands teenagers. This seems so obvious, but our knowledge of the teenage brain has evolved in recent times, with many of our traditional assumptions suddenly under scrutiny and up for debate (Epstein 2007; Lorain 2002; Reyna and Farley 2006; Underwood 2006).

Research that uses magnetic resonance imaging (MRI) technology to track the blood flow in the brain during various stimuli demonstrates a clear difference between the response of the teenage brain and the adult brain. In addition, Jay Giedd (Giedd et al. 2009) has employed MRI technology since 1991 to map brain development and has demonstrated that the development of the brain can occur up to the age of 25, well past the age once thought. Indeed, it was once believed that the brain was near fully developed in the early years of a child's life. The work of people such as Dr. Spock was predicated on this belief. Well-intentioned parents crammed education into their children to beat this clock. It is true that most brain development does occur during this early period, with most synapses established, but it does not mean that substantial development does not occur later, as recent research suggests.

Scientific research has tracked two processes that occur over time in the development of the teenage brain: *arborization*, which is the development of the gray matter of the brain by the creation of new dendrites, and *regressive pull*, which balances arborization through the competitive development of some gray matter while other areas are sacrificed.

The quantity of gray matter usually peaks during ages 12–13, after which the amount of white matter increases. At this point, myelination (the sheathing of neurons in insulation to improve performance) occurs. This process is dynamic and allows the early teenage brain to adjust to its environment. As stated earlier, this process continues until age 25.

Between brain development, changing hormonal makeup, and environmental stimuli, there can be no doubt about what adults have known for years by experience: Teenagers are different. The researchers may debate the issue on the relative effect of the three factors, but the end results are indisputable.

So, what have the researchers learned, and how does it affect our approach to teaching? It is all about recognizing and adapting to behaviors displayed by teens.

### *Teenagers Process Emotions Differently.*

Indeed, they seem to process their emotions in a different part of the brain than adults do. They find it more difficult to interpret body language, speech, and facial expressions correctly. Researchers suggest that this is the reason they are more likely to clash with their peers over issues that never would cause conflicts between adults.

Teachers need to recognize these tendencies when arbitrating disputes between students. Guidance of the disputing parties is the key, as the teacher may have to take the lead in making both parties recognize the real cause of the dispute. Staying calm is crucial, as the teacher must also take the lead in tamping down emotions. It is never a good idea for the teacher to over-react, which might aggravate the dispute.

### *Teenagers Have a Difficult Time Working During Times of Heightened Emotion.*

Studies demonstrate that if a student learns a lesson under emotional duress, they are less likely to remember the lesson later. Teachers must constantly monitor the behavior of their students and be aware of their emotional state. On days where extreme distress (or happiness) is evident, some flexibility in expectations by the teacher is prudent. This can be a challenge early in a class where the teacher has not had much time to observe students' normal behavior patterns. At this stage in getting to know students, teachers must be observers of both work habits and behavior to establish a baseline.

### *The Sleep Cycle Changes Drastically for Teenagers.*

A child who had no problems going to bed early and getting up early suddenly cannot go to sleep until a later hour and becomes difficult to wake up in the morning. Given that we force these teens to awake earlier than their brains want them to, the result is that teenagers are often sleep deprived. This causes students to forget 20–30% of what they learn due to loss of REM sleep, when the brain does much of the integration of new information.

It is one irony of our modern education system that these teenagers, who are now in need of more sleep in the morning, are often the first ones in school in the morning. This policy is driven by issues of safety for younger students, but it flies in the face of this new understanding of the teenage brain. It partially explains the frustration teachers often feel when students forget lessons from the previous day.

There is little that a high school teacher can do to change the education system in which they work, but understanding this phenomenon can be used to refine expectations and drive reteaching of material. It should also cause adjustments of curriculum pace to compensate. Teachers can also work with parents to encourage their kids to slow down in the evenings earlier and catch up on their sleep on weekends.

### *Sleep Deprivation Increases the Risk of Developing Depression in Teenagers.*

Given that many mental health problems develop in the teenage years, this must be a serious concern for teachers and other professionals involved in the lives of these students. Teachers must constantly monitor their students for changes in behavior or work quality that may signal the onset of depression or more serious ailments. Concerns should be expressed promptly to counselors or principals if a teacher believes a student has mental health problems.

### *Teenagers Exhibit a Propensity Toward Experimentation and Risk Taking.*

Any adult who has been exposed to teenagers knows this without the help of researchers. Teenagers are more likely than younger students or adults to experiment with alcohol or drugs, have unprotected sex, drive under the influence, and dabble in dangerous activities. Some researchers believe this is a natural process that is part of the teenagers' forming identities. Still, it is imperative that adults, including teachers, monitor these proclivities and respond accordingly to keep harm from occurring to the teenager or the people around them.

An additional concern for teachers is the effect of drugs and alcohol on learning. Some research suggests that drugs and alcohol damage the ability to memorize and learn in the hippocampus of a teenager's brain. This should motivate teachers to be especially vigilant in observing signs of drug and alcohol abuse in the student population.

As stated earlier, there is some debate about whether these findings are better explained by brain development or exposure to a particular environment. There is some evidence that environment may trump simple brain development, because teenagers in Eastern cultures display somewhat different behaviors. But from a pragmatic standpoint, the cause is not important. High school teachers still need to keep the resulting behaviors in mind when performing their duties and interacting with students.

## What About the Effect on Learning?

Research clearly shows that brains continue to develop well after what was once considered the brain's development period. Even more important for learning is that the rate of development will vary with the individual. This means students will develop their abilities in higher-order thinking in their own time.

What does this mean to the teacher? The teacher must be more flexible and provide scaffolding of the lessons when necessary. Now that we know the truth about brain development, we must guard against the usual rigid expectations of higher-order abilities at a given age so that we do not frustrate and damage the confidence of a student just because nature has decided the student will gain cognitive abilities later than his or her peers. Teachers must assist the natural development by providing tools and methods (discussed later) that promote it in an environment that allows students to stumble without consequences. Finally, teachers must be patient and provide encouragement as the natural process takes place.

Here are some specific suggestions for teachers:

- *Place comments on homework and classwork without a numerical grade so that students can learn without the fear of failure.* Confidence is important and fragile. By de-emphasizing grades during the early learning process of a unit, students are free to make mistakes and learn from them without fear getting in the way. In addition, students are more likely to ask questions and make progress toward mastery when fear of grades is not a factor.
- *Use oral quizzing (no grades) to assess the degree to which a student can perform functions of higher-order processing.* Nothing is more valuable for the assessment of higher-order skills than probing questions while the student performs learning tasks. Teachers should direct the questions in a way that assesses the student's ability to be systematic, see relevant patterns, conclude from data and calculations, and break complex problems into smaller units. The teacher can then guide the student toward incremental improvement of these abilities.
- *Grade for improvement and mastery.* This change in philosophy provides assessment while acknowledging the variability of brain development. It requires a degree of flexibility and new thinking that many teachers find difficult to accept. Still, if our goal is to get the best out of each and every student we teach, the variability of brain development must be accounted for in assessment.
- *Use the methods in this book to enhance and accelerate the development of higher-order thinking skills.* Although the brain's development rate is unique to an individual, the teacher can still provide tools to enhance and accelerate the process. This book provides tools to build a student's ability to see patterns, systematize their thinking, conclude from data and analysis, and break down complex problems into a series of simple problems. These are critical skills for building higher-order thinking abilities.

## References

Epstein, R. 2007. The myth of the teen brain. *Scientific American Mind*, April/May, 56–63.

Giedd, J. N., F. M. Lalonde, M. J. Celano, S. L. White, G. L. Wallace, N. R. Lee, and R. K. Lenroot. 2009. Anatomical brain magnetic resonance imaging of typically developing children and adolescents. *Journal of the American Academy of Child Adolescent Psychiatry* 48 (5): 465–470.

Lorain, P. 2002. Brain development in young adolescents. National Education Association. *www.nea.org/tools/16653.htm*.

Reyna V., and F. Farley. 2006. Is the teen brain too rational? *Scientific American Mind*, December, 58–65.

Underwood, N. 2006. The teenage brain: Why adolescents sleep in, take risks and won't listen to reason. *The Walrus*, November. *www.walrusmagazine.com/articles/2006.11-science-the-teenage-brain*.

# CHAPTER 2

# Conquering Culture and Psychology

## I Remember My Physics or Precalculus Course in High School or College ... Shudder!

How many physical science teachers or higher-level math teachers have heard something like this when asked what they teach? If you have spent any time teaching subjects such as chemistry, physics, precalculus, calculus, or another advanced math or science subject, someone has said something like this to you, followed by the always embarrassing "You must be really smart" comment. People are often surprised that science and mathematics teachers can hold a conversation with "normal people," and that they have interests in areas such as sports or the arts as well.

This attitude toward math and science is prolific enough that it has created its own culture and stereotype. People who are good at math, science, or computers are referred to as nerds or geeks and thought of as computer-obsessed, pocket-protected social outcasts. We see this stereotype perpetuated and reinforced throughout our culture in the form of literature and cinema characters (*Revenge of the Nerds*) and in school social stations. Where does this all come from?

Fact: There is a substantial amount of fear of mathematics and science in the general population that drives and maintains these attitudes (Geist 2010; Kaplan 2010; Sparks 2011; Tobias 1995). Despite a push by industry and the government to improve student mastery and retention of these two important subjects, students often start these courses with preconceived notions of the difficulty of the material, the social implications of pursuing these subjects, and the applicability of the subjects to their lives. This attitude often stems from stories and attitudes expressed to the students by adults, fellow students, and the media before they even enter the class. Even some teachers, victims of math and science anxiety themselves, have contributed to student apprehension. This is especially true of girls, where a study by the University of Chicago has suggested that female teachers often pass their math anxiety on to their female students.

Whatever the reasons, teachers find themselves fighting from the first day of class against the urban legends, stereotypes, and culture of fear that seem to perpetuate generation after generation.

## Did the Problem Originate With the Material? The Teaching Methods? The Teachers?

Actually, it's a bit of all three.

There is no doubt that science and mathematics courses can be challenging; they should be. Beyond the mastery of the subject, these courses provide some of the first opportunities to hone higher-order thinking skills in problem solving and analysis. Even if a student has no intention of pursuing a science- or mathematics-based career, these mastered thinking skills provide a foundation that will assist the student in later academic and professional life, regardless of career goals.

Still, there is that challenge of the underlying fear of mathematics and science from a skills perspective that must be understood and dealt with adequately. Table 2.1 displays a table of typical units within various mathematics and physical science courses.

**TABLE 2.1**

Typical Units in Mathematics and Physical Science Courses

| Subject | Units |
|---|---|
| Algebra | • Functions and graphs, domain/range, roots<br>• Solution of linear equations for a variable using commutative, distributive, and associative properties and inverse functions<br>• Functions and their graphs from parent functions<br>• Linear functions and graphs, slope, and $y$-intercept<br>• Solving and graphing quadratic equations by factoring, completing the square, and using the quadratic formula<br>• Solving systems of equations<br>• Simplifying expressions with exponents and roots<br>• Solving and graphing polynomial equations<br>• Solving and graphing rational functions<br>• Solving and graphing expressions with logarithms and exponentials |

**TABLE 2.1** *(continued)*

| Subject | Units |
|---|---|
| Geometry | • Proofs of theorems<br>• Intersecting lines and segments<br>• Parallel lines and transversals<br>• Properties of triangles and quadrilaterals<br>• Congruency and similarity<br>• Geometry with chords and circles<br>• Solving algebraic geometry problems<br>• Areas, perimeters, and volumes of geometric figures<br>• Geometry on coordinate systems, length, and midpoint formulas<br>• Constructions and transformations of geometric figures |
| Precalculus | • Roots, extrema, and asymptotes of functions<br>• Composite and combination functions<br>• Functions and their relationship with a parent function<br>• Trigonometric, inverse trigonometric, exponential, logarithmic, absolute value, rational functions, and polynomial functions<br>• Radial coordinates<br>• Trigonometric identities<br>• Conic sections<br>• Series and sequences, sums<br>• Parametric equations<br>• Vectors<br>• Complex numbers |
| Calculus | • Limits of series<br>• Derivatives of basic functions<br>• Derivatives of functions using chain rule, product rule, and quotient rule<br>• Applying derivatives to finding of extrema of functions<br>• Indefinite and definite integrals of basic functions<br>• Definite and indefinite integration by applying basic forms, variable change, trigonometric substitution, integration by parts, reduction formula, trigonometric identities, and partial fractions<br>• Applying integrals to finding function areas and volumes of rotation<br>• Differential equations |

**TABLE 2.1** *(continued)*

| Subject | Units |
|---|---|
| Chemistry | • Laboratory methods<br>• Chemical change vs. physical change<br>• Compounds vs. mixtures<br>• Atomic structure and quantum mechanics<br>• Bonding<br>• Molecular shape and crystals<br>• Reaction balancing and stoichiometry<br>• Empirical and molecular formulas<br>• Kinetic theory and gas laws<br>• Reaction thermodynamics<br>• Reaction rates<br>• Chemical equilibrium of reversible reactions<br>• Solutions<br>• Acid and base theories<br>• Oxidation-reduction reactions<br>• Electrochemistry<br>• Nuclear reactions |
| Physics | • Laboratory methods<br>• Kinematics<br>• Vector mathematics<br>• Forces and Newton's laws<br>• Circular motion and universal gravitation<br>• Harmonic motion<br>• Work, energy, and power, machines<br>• Momentum and impulse<br>• Rotational motion<br>• Fluid mechanics<br>• Thermodynamics (material effects, heat, heat transfer, and processes)<br>• Waves, sound, light, and optics<br>• Electricity and magnetism, circuits<br>• Quantum mechanics<br>• Atomic and nuclear physics<br>• Relativity |

Many of these skills are daunting for students and must be addressed with care from a fear perspective. Insufficient mastery of some of the skills within these units can cause problems in later coursework, in which some of these skills would be treated as prerequisites. Fear, however, can often cause students to give up when learning the material if sufficient scaffolding and encouragement are not in place as part of the lesson.

In mathematics, students often struggle with algebra and geometry, never attaining sufficient mastery while taking these courses. It is no wonder that students often deal with significant trepidation when faced with higher-level mathematics and science courses later in their studies.

In the sciences, physics is a particularly fearsome subject for many students. It is often the first time students are asked to apply their acquired higher-level math skills to multistep application problems. Students must develop and hone their higher-order thinking skills in problem solving and analysis while perfecting the necessary mathematics skills. In addition, students must hone their skills in the analysis of data sets from laboratories and the ability to draw conclusions from the data.

The challenge to the teacher is to take students beyond the fear of and attitudes toward the material to see the big picture—how it can be relevant to their interests and their future goals, and that difficult does not have to mean impossible or boring. Teachers need to direct the lessons to allow exploration of the subject within the interests, learning styles, and capabilities of the student.

Regardless of the prevailing attitudes, lessons that are fun tend to be the most successful. This poses a challenge to teachers to provide lessons that promote the mastery of concepts and still keep the most intimidated or attitude-challenged student engaged. Wrapping a lesson in a competitive game between individual students or student groups can replace fear of the difficult with the challenges of the game. Providing a tangible reward for success in the game is even better. Anyone who has ever watched a child play video games or compete in sports knows they will work on the skills to master them. The fact is, students do not shy away from challenges if they perceive them as fun or cool.

Teaching must be executed with an attitude of nurturing that allows students to explore the subject without trepidation and stumble without fear of repercussions. Teachers need to understand that students reach mastery of problem solving and analytical thinking skills at different rates and with different levels of difficulty. This is normal, but it is a fact often ignored in the design of lessons and assessments.

What we must stop doing as teachers is enforcing the traditional culture of rigidity that breeds fear and loathing of the subject. There has been a cultural norm in science and math education that failure is normal and even desirable. Some science and mathematics teachers have even expressed that they actually judge themselves by how high their failure rate is!

Teachers have been using the same basic lessons for generations with only minor modifications and thus have perpetuated the problem. There is often an arrogance in the science and mathematics teaching community that suggests these two subjects are supposed to separate the weaker students from the stronger ones. These teachers express this attitude by making formal testing and laboratory reports the only forms of assessment and then grading them rigidly. Students often develop a fear of being wrong from these graded assessments that carry over to every activity in the classroom. At this point, the teacher has engrained a fear in the student that he or she often carries into future courses. These are elitist and counterproductive attitudes that have chased away many students who might have developed an interest in mathematics or science before they developed the higher-order skills required for mastery or learned subject matter that might have fostered their interest.

As teachers, we must stress to our students the difference between the concepts of difficult and impossible. We must encourage our students to embrace challenges the way coaches make their players embrace and conquer challenges on playing fields or music directors make students master a difficult piece of music. Students need to be made to buy into their own education in mathematics and science and approach their studies with diligence and patience.

## Dr. LaFave, How Will This Ever Be Relevant to My Life?

I wish I had a dollar for every time a student has asked me this question. Some teachers take offense when faced with this question, as if it should be obvious how much the student needs to learn what he or she is teaching. That attitude drives a wedge in the relationship between the teacher and student and fails to acknowledge an important point.

Teachers need to take the lead in answering this question, even if a student is asking it to be amusing (or annoying). It really isn't a bad question. How can you force a student to care about physics, for instance, if you can't tell him when or why he would ever use it or why he should appreciate it?

It is useful to discuss this query on the first class day, asking each student about their career goals and then relating the subject matter to those goals. This discussion is then followed by curriculum design that will reinforce the connection. Sometimes the answer to the question is easy. For students that aspire to careers in science or engineering, the connections to mathematics and science courses are obvious and the traditional curriculum suffices. But for other career goals, the connection can be more tenuous or indirect.

A student who aspires to the arts or trades may not see a reason to spend time learning mathematics and science, but there are definite connections that can be made. As a prompt for teachers in discussions with these students, Table 2.2—which relates mathematics and science to the skills necessary for trades—and Table 2.3 (p. 15)—which relates mathematics and science to the skills necessary for athletics and the arts—should be displayed for the students.

**TABLE 2.2**

The Need for Mathematics and Sciences in the Trades

| Trade | Mathematics- and Science-Related Skills |
|---|---|
| Carpenter | • **Algebra:** calculation of material quantities and costs (linear equation solution)<br>• **Geometry:** framing and squaring of structures (parallel and perpendicular lines, angles); cutting random corners (angles); laying tile (Pythagorean theorem); leveling foundations (planes), estimates of construction material quantities (areas and volumes); reading blueprints (similarity and transformation)<br>• **Physics:** tool operation (machines); material strength and thermal properties (strength and thermal properties of solids); fastener operation (machines); insulation choice (heat transfer) |
| Cosmetologist | • **Chemistry:** pH of bleaches and dyes (acids and bases); skin and hair treatment reaction incompatibilities and toxicity (chemical reactions); makeup and cleanser properties (solutions, colligative properties, colloids, viscosity, evaporation)<br>• **Physics:** hair properties, strength, brittleness, elasticity (properties of solids); porosity |
| Electrician and electrical technician, network technician | • **Algebra:** calculation of currents, voltages, power, and energy for DC and AC circuits (linear and quadratic equation solution)<br>• **Geometry:** nodes and paths (points and segments)<br>• **Precalculus:** alternating circuits (trigonometric functions, vectors)<br>• **Calculus:** time-dependent currents and voltages (trigonometric functions, exponentials, differential equations)<br>• **Chemistry:** material conductivity (properties of metals and ions)<br>• **Physics:** resistance and conductivity (resistivity, Ohm's law); AC and DC circuits, current, and voltage (Kirchoff's laws, switches, capacitance, induction); heating and lighting (energy conversion, power); energy storage in capacitor and inductor fields (electric and magnetic fields, electric potential) |

**TABLE 2.2** *(continued)*

| Trade | Mathematics- and Science-Related Skills |
|---|---|
| Heating and cooling technician | • **Algebra:** heat transfer expressions (solving algebraic equations, polynomial)<br>• **Geometry:** heated or cooled volumes (volume), conduction and radiation calculations (lengths and areas)<br>• **Calculus:** energy consumption over time (integration)<br>• **Chemistry:** coolants, combustion (thermal chemistry); density<br>• **Physics:** radiators (radiative heat transfer); conduction and insulation (thermal conductivity); heating and cooling cycles (thermal processes); convection cycles in air and water (convection); water and coolant flow (fluid mechanics) |
| Machinist | • **Algebra:** calculation of part dimensions, mass properties (solution of algebraic equations)<br>• **Geometry:** CAD and blueprints (general geometry skills)<br>• **Calculus:** mass properties (integration)<br>• **Chemistry:** alloys (mixtures), mass, density<br>• **Physics:** material properties (mass properties, strength, elasticity, malleability, ductility, thermal); machine operation (work and power) |
| Automobile mechanic | • **Algebra:** solving general expressions for mechanics and thermodynamics<br>• **Geometry:** cylinder volume and piston area<br>• **Calculus:** work calculation on pistons (integration)<br>• **Chemistry:** combustion (thermal chemistry); density<br>• **Physics:** general mechanics (kinematics, statics and dynamics, machines, rotational motion); material properties (strength and thermal properties of solids); radiators (radiation heat transfer); conduction and insulation (thermal conductivity); machine cycles (pressure, thermal processes, P-V diagrams); water and coolant flow (fluid mechanics); lubricants (viscosity) |
| Plumber | • **Algebra:** calculation of pressures and flow rates (linear and quadratic equation solution)<br>• **Geometry:** nodes and flow paths (points and segments)<br>• **Chemistry:** material conductivity (properties of metals and ions)<br>• **Physics:** water flow in pipes (pressure, density, Bernoulli's equation, continuity equation, flow rate, viscosity); valves and pumps (machines) |

## TABLE 2.3

### The Need for Mathematics and Sciences in Athletics and the Arts

| Artist or Athlete | Mathematics- and Science-Related Skills |
|---|---|
| Athlete or dancer | • **Algebra:** basic algebra skills<br>• **Geometry:** play planning and choreography (general geometry skills); force application geometry<br>• **Chemistry:** nutrition (digestion reactions); medications, preparations<br>• **Physics:** body kinematics, statics, and dynamics (kinematics, statics and dynamics, rotational motion work, energy, and power) |
| Graphic artist, painter, or designer | • **Algebra:** basic algebra skills<br>• **Geometry:** perspective (angles and scaling, transformation); lighting direction; scaling and deformation (transformation)<br>• **Chemistry:** paint and media mixture and dilution (solutions, viscosity, suspensions, and colloids)<br>• **Physics:** color mixing; lighting (illumination); reflection and refraction of light |
| Sculptor or potter | • **Algebra:** basic algebra skills<br>• **Geometry:** all geometry skills<br>• **Chemistry:** chemical properties of media and glazes (chemical surface etching with acids, thermochemical properties); clay preparation (viscosity); etching chemicals (acids and bases); surface oxidation<br>• **Physics:** physical properties of media (mass, density, strength, flexibility, malleability, ductility); thermal properties of media (thermal expansion, evaporation); tools (work and machines) |
| Musician or singer<br>Sound technician | • **Algebra:** basic algebra skills<br>• **Geometry:** resonant cavity geometry; material dimensions<br>• **Precalculus:** sound waves (trigonometric functions and properties); loudness (logarithms)<br>• **Calculus:** energy usage (integration)<br>• **Chemistry:** material conductivity (properties of metals and ions)<br>• **Physics:** music theory—loudness, pitch, resonance, timbre and spectrum, consonance, dissonance, noise (longitudinal wave theory and properties); instrument material properties (elasticity); music and electronics (circuits, sound-to-electricity conversion, equalization of spectrum) |
| Fashion designer | • **Algebra:** material estimates (basic algebra skills)<br>• **Geometry:** dress pattern (similarity and transformation)<br>• **Chemistry:** dye mixing (solution); material absorption of dyes and glues; material safety—toxicity, flammability<br>• **Physics:** dye color mixing (color mixing); fiber and material properties (tensile strength, flexibility) |

Neither figure is meant to be all-encompassing, but rather to provide a basis for demonstrating to students who aspire to enter these fields that knowledge of mathematics and science is important to fulfilling their aspirations.

For instance, for a student who wants to study music, a strong connection can be made between wave mechanics and music theory. For a student who wants to paint, the physics of mixing colors or the science of reflection and refraction of light can be introduced.

There are an amazing number of publications available about mathematics and science for the trades and arts that the teacher can direct students to for enlightenment and inspiration (Bruter 2002; Dunlap 1992; Fauvel, Wilson, and Flood 2006; Herman 2007; Moore 2008; Ohio Math Work 2000; Smith 2007; Webster and Judy 2001).

Even more interesting connections can be made to the world of creative composition in art and music on the web, music sources, movie sources, and multimedia to further inspire the students. Bathsheba Grossman (Bathsheba Sculpture LLC 2011), a modern sculptor, uses computer-aided design (CAD) and fast prototyping methods for metal to produce intriguing sculptures based on geometric and physical concepts. Figure 2.1 displays two of her sculptures that are based on geometric and topological ideas.

Students who love music are often surprised to find that mathematical concepts such as fractals, statistical data, and field measurements can be used to actually compose music. This algorithmic approach to music has been pioneered by artists such as Brian Eno and Clarence Barlow. Modern electronic dance music by artists such as the Chemical Brothers and the Crystal Method uses a variety of technologies in the music's composition and performance. Finally, modern moviemaking has embraced a variety of technologies that encompass the mathematical and scientific world of computer generated imagery (CGI) techniques. CGI has allowed new and stunning visuals in movies that were not feasible a couple of decades ago.

For students who aspire to careers in business or the humanities, the benefits may have to be stressed in the form of indirect relationships, such as the enhancement of critical and analytical thinking. Analysis and problem solving are not the sole venue of the scientist or engineer, but are found throughout a variety of professional careers, from law to business management. For these students, an effort can be made during the course of study to pepper the curriculum with discussions of business problem solving and historical perspectives, science and mathematics in literature, or discussions of ethical issues.

There are some career goals that require a fair amount of imagination by the teacher to make a connection; however, an early effort to address the issue often sets a positive tone for future learning. Knowing a student's interests allows the teacher to adapt the lessons so that these connections are made clear to the student throughout the school year. Projects tailored to the student's interests are a particularly effective method for making this connection. It also allows the student to see how a lesson applies to everyday life.

**FIGURE 2.1**

Mathematics-Based Sculpture

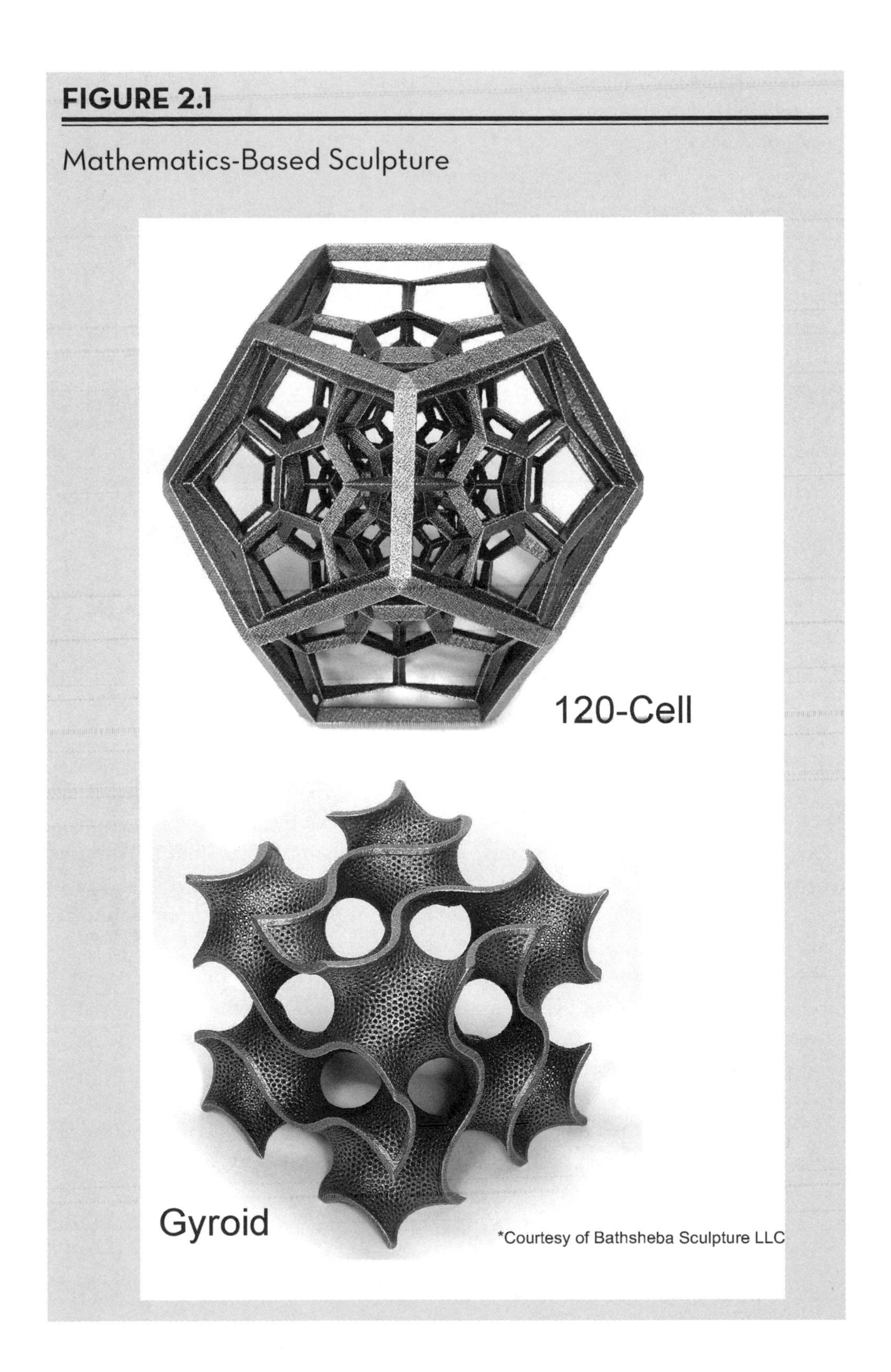

In some cases, it might also be necessary to alter the material emphasis for some students away from mathematical problem solving and toward a conceptual approach because calculating quantities might not be of great value for these students.

## Actively Observing Students Is Essential.

One proven methodology for promoting mastery and building confidence is the active observation of the working student. Whether the student is answering a concept question, working a problem, or performing or writing a lab, naive conceptions and sticking points occur at the most unexpected times and on the least-expected concepts. Appendix A (p. 143) displays a list of common student naive conceptions in physics based on a list compiled by Dr. Richard Olenick at The University of Texas at Dallas. Teachers of physics and physical science can use this list as a guide for what to be aware of when observing students' work. It is not uncommon for teachers to miss these naïve conceptions until late in the process of delivering a learning unit, when the naive conception has become ingrained in the student's understanding of the concept or principle.

Active observation allows the teacher to catch and correct the naive conception right when it occurs, before it becomes ingrained in the student's mind. The best method is for the instructor to pose leading questions that allow the student to find and correct the naive conception by himself. This is extremely effective for mitigating the problem, as a student will remember those facts better because he discovered and corrected the naive conception.

Conversely, quizzes should act as a formative assessment to allow teachers to catch these problems before a summative assessment, but they are less than effective in many cases because too much time often goes by from the first signs of the naive conception until the grading of the quiz. Naive conceptions can propagate and ingrain themselves in the interim to a point that they become much more difficult to mitigate before the summative assessment is administered.

Once a naive conception is determined via active observation, what does the teacher do to remedy it? Page Keeley has done significant work in the area of formative assessment and naive conceptions. She makes the following points about naïve conceptions (Keeley 2008):

- Prior knowledge and experiences determine how students view a physical phenomenon or concept.
- Teaching is not learning.
- Formative assessment promotes thinking and elicits information about the thinking process.
- All ideas in a learning environment must be accepted and respected, not just the right ones.

- Selection and execution of formative assessments must be purposeful.
- Formative assessment results can be used to initiate inquiry and engage students in discussion.
- Contextual limits can inhibit students' grasp of major points.
- Hands-on activities can have unintended consequences.
- Representations of physical concepts and principles of phenomena can reinforce or initiate naive conceptions.
- Naive conceptions can be good if they are used to bridge a student's understanding of science concepts and principles with their initial ideas.

Based on these points, Keeley and associates have put together a set of 75 formative assessment probes—tools that explore a student's ideas about various scientific phenomena and concepts (Keeley, Eberle, and Farrin 2005; Keeley, Eberle, and Tugel 2007; Keeley, Eberle, and Dorsey 2008). Each probe starts with a specific guiding question about the nature of an event or object. The students' preconceived models of the nature of the phenomenon or concept, right or wrong, are used as a starting point for exploring the true nature of the phenomenon or concept. Exploration can be done using demonstrations, simulations, or observations to elicit discussions linking the specifics of the probe to the underlying physical principles while narrowing student viewpoints down to a correct explanation of the principles involved.

Each probe comes with teacher notes containing useful information to help the teacher guide the resulting discussion. This information contains explanations of the correct concepts and principles involved and specific research on the level of understanding and known naive conceptions that occur at the elementary, middle, and high school levels. It also presents links to related phenomena for follow-up discussions.

For example, one probe asks students to explain what is inside the bubbles they observe when water boils. The teacher's notes explain that the bubbles contain water vapor, another phase of water. A detailed explanation of the underlying processes of kinetic theory, evaporation, phase change, vapor pressure, and buoyancy is given to assist the teacher in guiding the discussion. Research on the level of understanding of the underlying principles for elementary, middle, and high school students is also given. It also explains that some students believe the bubbles contain heat, air, vacuum, or separated oxygen and hydrogen. All of this information in the teacher notes can help guide student discussion and mitigate naive conceptions.

These formative assessment probes are excellent tools to execute during or right after active observation. Students clear up their own naive conceptions, making it more likely that they will retain the correct explanation and build confidence.

### *Not Just Their Work But How They Work*

Teachers need to take the time to watch how a student performs a learning task. It is important for the student to be organized and develop systematic approaches to work in mathematics and science, especially with problem solving and laboratory work. It is rare for students to be neat and systematic without learning the corresponding techniques. Observing how a student works allows the teacher to make suggestions that will help the student develop good habits in his or her approach to the work.

Observation of students' work also gives insight into how they view their task. If students are getting off task, it may require a change of approach or learning style to meet their natural proclivities.

### *Don't Just Watch—Ask!*

Teachers should be active in their observation, not passive. Students will rarely volunteer information when they are struggling. Sometimes this is caused by embarrassment, or sometimes it can be due to apathy. Teachers need to watch for inactivity and ask leading questions to determine where a student is stuck or what he or she is considering, if anything. This can be a trial-and-error process to find questions that prompt the student to progress in the lesson without giving the answers.

It is important that teachers maintain patience in this active observation. It is easy to get impatient and give the student too much information, circumventing the self-exploration process that is so important for attaining mastery. Students will often push a teacher to lead them directly to the knowledge, but teachers must be steadfast in protecting the student-centered learning environment.

It is also important that the teacher exude encouragement and a positive attitude. Maintaining a level of confidence in a student is necessary to keep the student from giving up on the task. Classroom teachers know how fragile a child's confidence is but often fail to account for this in how they manage the classroom and learning environment. Failure to remain patient and positive can do permanent damage to any future academic progress. Teachers should tell students directly and often that they have confidence in them—especially students who are struggling. This simple act has been found to have a positive influence on a student's confidence.

## Remembering That the Material Is Challenging

It is a natural phenomenon for teachers to forget the difficulty of the material they are teaching. As we master material, we often look back and wonder how we ever found it difficult. This can taint a teacher's perspective and blind the teacher to the points in the material where students might struggle. The phenomenon can adversely affect lesson planning and assessment design.

A useful technique for reflection and future lesson development is to keep a journal of naive conceptions. As concepts in the lessons are discovered that students misunderstand or misapply, they may be written into the journal for that unit so that the teacher is aware the next time a lesson is given. This technique acts to remind the teacher what it was like to learn the lesson for the first time.

Teachers must also understand the importance of modeling, especially when teaching problem solving. In the first weeks of a difficult course such as physics or calculus, teachers need to model the correct processes for problem solving using many sample problems. This will help students learn how to organize information and execute processes when solving a problem. The student will begin to see the steps and commonalities within the set of examples and then use them in their own problem solving. In Chapter 5, we will present a complete systematic process for problem solving that should be applied to the modeling examples demonstrated by the teacher.

## The Problem of Insufficient Prerequisite Knowledge

One universal complaint from mathematics and science teachers is that students often come to class with insufficient mastery of the prerequisite material for the course. Nothing can derail the timescale of a curriculum like finding out your students do not know the necessary previous knowledge for the material you are teaching. The reasons for this phenomenon vary, and I won't get into a discussion of the reasons here. Instead, I want to address techniques for mitigating the resulting disruption to teaching the course material.

An important tool that can help teachers get a handle on the extent and characteristics of the problem is the preassessment. Giving a preassessment to students at the beginning of each unit allows the teacher to understand the degree of mastery of prerequisite knowledge and the specific deficiencies for each student. Teachers should not grade these assessments for any reason other than diagnostic purposes. It is not the purpose of this assessment to judge the student, but rather to assist them in mitigating any deficiencies.

These preassessments should be kept short and specific to the material of the unit. It is important that it be scored as quickly as possible (again, not as part of the formal grade), as this allows both the teacher and student to understand the nature and extent of their deficiencies. One technique that can be used is to allow the students to exchange papers and grade them as the teacher reviews the answers. The teacher can then collect the papers, review them, and return them to the students quickly for perusal. If available, the tests can be administered with electronic multiple choice systems or Scantrons, although this will not demonstrate the details of deficiencies. The teacher should examine the actual work leading to answers for questions answered incorrectly. Again, these grades should not be used for formal assessment toward a course grade; their use should be strictly diagnostic.

For maximum effectiveness, the test results should be returned to the students within one day. This allows time for mitigation of the deficiencies with minimal effect on the lesson timeline. Remember, the students should understand that the grades do not count toward their grade for the unit.

So, now that the deficiencies have been diagnosed, what does a teacher do to mitigate them? Whatever method is chosen, it is important that it not take too much time out of the teaching of the course material. One method is for the teacher to keep a bank of practice worksheets that can be given to students for homework, in tutoring sessions, or as warm-ups. These worksheets should be short and specific to particular deficiencies. Grades or other incentives can be given for completion of these worksheets.

It can be a daunting task for one teacher to formulate such a bank of worksheets. It is best done by teams of teachers working together. For science teachers, it would be prudent to consult with mathematics teachers on the formulation of worksheets dealing with math deficiencies.

## Building Habits

Maybe this section should have been called "Fixing Bad Habits." It is important that teachers be realistic about the behaviors of the students they teach. Students will tend toward doing the minimum when performing tasks, an especially big problem when teaching high school students. This tendency can be counterproductive when you are trying to get students to follow a uniform process (presented later in this book) because students tend to want to skip steps.

So, what can a teacher do to stop this tendency? One proven method is to give a grade for following the steps in the recipe. The downside of this is that it substantially increases the time needed to solve and grade a problem. To balance this, teachers should give a smaller number of problems on assignments and tests and spread the point values for the problem over all the steps of the recipe.

Other aspects of this tendency to do the minimum can be seen in inadequate note-taking, incomplete assignments, and off-task activities. As much as teachers would like to believe they can captivate their students at all times, they know in reality that even the best of students, under the most favorable conditions, will display these types of behaviors sometimes. Truth be told, these behaviors are probably worse in math and science classes, as it is impossible not to have lessons that, although important, are less than captivating to all students. One approach to mitigating this is to give grades for notebooks and classwork—anything to force the issue on developing good habits.

Teachers need to keep in mind that teaching good habits to their students—whether that is behavior, study skills, or organization—goes well beyond secondary school or the particular subject matter being taught. These habits become crucial in both collegiate and work endeavors, regardless of the details of their duties. Teachers need to take a broad perspective when considering the relative importance and relevance of study and organizational skills within their teaching and treat them as equally important as the subject matter in the student's development. A student may never apply the content of your course after leaving your classroom, but the study and organizational skills you provide will be important no matter what career path the the student takes.

## The Importance of Safety Nets

There is nothing more fragile than a student's confidence. It takes only a few failures for some students to throw in the towel and give up on themselves, a state from which they may never recover. Teachers see this behavior all the time, especially with high school students. Almost every teacher, especially high school teachers, has a story of a student who quit on himself or herself. Unfortunately, sometimes students enter a class already believing they will fail. Teachers, especially in mathematics and the physical sciences, face no more daunting task than to balance challenging their students with maintaining, or even reviving, their confidence levels.

Meeting this challenge often requires a change of perspective by the teacher toward grading and even what constitutes success. Teachers need to keep in mind that their subject matter has different relevance to different students, and some students may struggle with the material for a variety of reasons, such as insufficient prerequisite skills and knowledge, immature higher-order thinking skills, or insufficient study skills. There must be a balance in grading that values both mastery and improvement so that students with different academic strengths and interests or immature higher-order thinking skills may find their own levels of success with the material. Couple this system with a classroom environment that promotes encouragement, and teachers can keep from sacrificing those students to a complete loss of confidence. The cost of maintaining the "traditional mastery first" environment can be to lose some students early before they have a chance to meet their academic potential.

## Remembering That the Subject Is Not Important to All Students

This may be a hard notion for some educators to admit to, but not all students will find their class exciting or worthwhile, no matter what effort the teacher makes to captivate them. Unfortunately, for teachers in core subjects, students often don't choose to enroll in the class but are placed there to meet graduation and college entrance requirements. Some students may see no relevance of the subject to their future goals. This means there will always be a portion of the class who will come in with less than the best attitudes and the teacher will have to teach them anyway. The challenges of this situation are familiar to any experienced teacher.

Again, teaching these students successfully can require a change of attitude and perspective by the teacher. There is nothing wrong with these students other than that their interests and goals lie in a different direction, away from science and mathematics. Sometimes they have naive conceptions about the applicability of the subject and must be enlightened (see Tables 2.2 and 2.3, pp. 13–15), but other times there is indeed no nontrivial applicability to be found. Teachers often misinterpret the lack of interest by these students as a sign of disrespect or bad behavior and respond in a counterproductive manner. Teachers must recognize that there will be students in the class who will require a different approach to teach successfully.

To teach these students, great care must be taken to try to connect lessons to their interests whenever possible. Demonstrations and presentations of unusual phenomenon, or historical or current events discussions, can be used to intrigue these students and promote curiosity. Projects that connect the material to the known interests of students, directly or indirectly, can be a good approach to successfully educating these students. Students can use their natural interests in history, literature, art, multimedia, or dramatic presentation to connect to the subject material through projects that integrate these interests.

Given that some students may not use the subject matter in their chosen occupation later, the teacher will have to alter his or her goals with this type of student. A conceptual approach to the subject that promotes basic understanding or appreciation of the material may be the better approach for these students, rather than a rigorous approach that stresses problem solving and analysis. Teachers must find a way to make the subject interesting, despite the lack of relevancy, while allowing for some avenue of measurable student success.

## Caring for Your Students: Building Trust and Confidence

When a student enters a classroom with damaged confidence, it can be quite a challenge for a teacher to re-establish this confidence. These students often exhibit rebellious or apathetic attitudes so that they don't feel like failures; essentially, they give up on themselves and justify it with false bravado or apathy. This behavior can become especially acute in an advanced science or mathematics class, as the students often struggle most in these subjects and come in with preconceived fears of the material.

Experienced teachers know that the problem often goes well beyond an individual student. The rebellious nature exhibited by these students can often disrupt an entire classroom learning environment. Amazingly, it can take just one student with this problem, properly motivated (or unmotivated, depending on your perspective), to effectively stymie the learning environment. This effect is the cause of many classroom management issues and teacher frustrations.

This question must be addressed for this situation: How does a teacher instruct this kind of student effectively, keep the student from disrupting the whole class, and maintain his or her own sanity? A survey of teachers concerning this and other issues demonstrates this to be a major source of concern for many. One common reaction to this situation is for teachers to give up on the student. Given the challenges and stresses of modern education, this is somewhat understandable; however, it is not appropriate or professional to do so. Teachers need to use experience, resources, and creativity to attempt to reach these students and provide avenues of success for them. Will teachers be able to reach all of these students? The answer is probably no; however, it is important that an attempt be made to bring all students up to their potential. With some effort and planning, it should be possible to have some reasonable level of success with these students.

One effective strategy can be executed on the first day of class by establishing a positive relationship with the students at the beginning. The time taken to get to know your students personally can yield savings in time and aggravation later and provide a foundation for the teacher to re-establish confidence. Teachers should take the time that first day to learn their students' interests and goals and find out what activities they are involved in both inside and outside the school. Demonstrating a genuine interest in and enthusiasm for a student's activities and dreams can elicit a firm foundation of respect and goodwill in return. To maximize the effectiveness of this approach, this process should be undertaken before you set the classroom rules. It will have a larger psychological impact if you start the relationship with a positive discussion rather than a negative one.

Once the teacher has set this positive tone for the relationship, the relationship must be nurtured. If the teachers don't reinforce this relationship, the effect of that first day will drop off as the weeks of the course proceed. There are several tactics that have been found to work well.

### *Go to Student Shows, Sporting Events, and Activities.*

It isn't necessary for the teacher to attend every student event at the school, but making time to be seen at activities students care about lets the students know you have a genuine interest in them. Even the most disruptive of students find it hard to say no to a teacher who takes the time to attend their activities. Teachers may find this to be the best classroom management strategy they can use.

Teachers should spread their time over many activities: athletics, music, arts, and so on. This should not be looked at purely as a classroom-management ploy. Teachers may find attending these activities to be quite enjoyable. If you are a teacher who hasn't attended your students' shows and activities, you are missing out on one of the true joys of being a teacher.

Make sure you find your students during or after activities to give them encouragement and express how much you enjoyed the activity. This reinforces your goal and can mean more to them than you can imagine. This is especially important with some students from at-risk environments where the parents may not be able to attend the activities themselves. Your presence and encouragement often have the largest positive effect on these students.

### Encourage Activity.

Find out the talent set of a student, match him to a school activity, and then encourage him to participate. Some students tend to avoid school activities, even when they match well with their talents and interests. By executing this strategy, teachers are demonstrating a true interest in the student while getting her into an activity that can have a positive influence on her life. Fact: Students who are involved in activities tend to perform better academically. The teacher should follow up this effort to encourage the student by attending an event of her activity.

### Become an Activity or Club Sponsor.

Nothing proves to students that you care about them like volunteering your time and effort to sponsor a school activity or club. It is proof to the students that you aren't just talking about caring about them. Teachers may find that this effort not only reinforces the positive relationship but also can be quite rewarding for the teacher.

### Be a Good Listener and Mentor.

Let the student speak and be a good listener. You can learn a tremendous amount about your students this way. Students often deal with issues inside and outside school that many teachers cannot even imagine. These issues can have a real negative effect on academic performance. At-risk students are especially vulnerable to these negative influences.

An excellent method for maintaining a positive relationship between teacher and students is to let the students know they can come to you to talk. You may not be able to solve their problems (often you will not), but the act of listening with compassion can often lessen their stress and strengthen trust and respect. Note that there are issues they may come to you with where you will be forced to act (child abuse being one such issue). Make sure you handle these kinds of issues with particular care and compassion and within the law and school policies.

Some schools have mentoring programs. This is an excellent way for a teacher to establish this link with students in an organized fashion, with some training to allow the teacher to handle more sensitive issues.

### Greet Your Students With a Smile and a Greeting at the Door Every Day.

It seems like a small thing, but starting each day off this way establishes a positive attitude right from the start. My students have told me that they look forward to this informal time with me. Short chats with the students before class can further reinforce the personal relationship you have established.

### *Make Positive Calls to Parents.*

Many teachers have only one positive conversation with parents: at the open house at the beginning of term. After that, calls to parents have been relegated to issues of performance deficiencies and bad behavior. This needs to be changed. An effective way to build a positive relationship with a student is to call the parents to give them good reports on their children. Visible changes in the attitudes and performance of children have been observed after such a phone call. In addition, it establishes a good rapport with the parents if unpleasant issues do arise.

You get a real feel for how many times a teacher has called to report a negative issue when you get a parent on the telephone. Most parents automatically believe that a teacher call means trouble. They are often a bit confused when you give them good news. Parents will often ask what the bad news is after the good news is given, fully expecting that the good news was just provided to soften the effect of the bad news.

Teachers need to be creative and flexible in defining successes for some students. For students whose confidence is especially damaged and who see themselves as failures, the teacher may have to celebrate the small successes. But it isn't that difficult. Even the worst students have good days that you can use when reporting to parents. Improvement in performance or behavior by a student is an excellent occurrence to report to their parents.

Note that teachers should make this communication via a phone call rather than an e-mail or text message. The personal touch reinforces the message more effectively. In addition, heaping praise on the student directly, in conjunction with the parent call, can magnify the positive effect.

### *Use Reinforcement as the Last Resort.*

Teachers who have used this method know that it works, and it is supported by recent brain research (Tarko 2006). Even the most difficult student will often fall in line for a piece of candy or other incentive. There is no one more mercenary than a child. Even when the future benefits of education are explained to them, they will often respond to immediate payoff much more effectively than the potential for future benefits. Many teachers find this kind of paying for learning to be distasteful, and there is plenty of debate over the long-term effectiveness. However, sometimes it is better to choose pragmatism over certain failure.

For this system to work, some rules should be followed:

- The learning and achievement goals that need to be satisfied to receive the incentive should be set upfront and unambiguous to all involved.
- Teachers need to be rigid about expectations. Be sure that assignments are done within deadlines and are of sufficient quality. Students need to earn the rewards.
- An occasional surprise reward for some small achievement outside the set goals can often enhance the effectiveness of the program.

- Reward the student promptly upon achieving a set goal. Nothing can derail the system faster than reneging on a promised incentive.

It should be noted that we are not advocating bribes. The reward should never be given before the task is completed. Bribes are rarely effective in guaranteeing compliance.

Also, teachers do need to be careful about using sweets as a prize. Some school districts have rules against this. In addition, care must be taken to make sure the student doesn't have a health issue that can be aggravated by sugar. As an alternative, teachers may give small toys, privileges, or other rewards as incentives. Many schools have established incentive programs that can be used for this purpose.

This approach has actually been championed and institutionalized by several schools under various programs involving monetary incentives. These schools are actually paying students for academic achievement, and the programs have had measurable success (Toppo 2008). The details change from program to program, but the schools find they get excellent results. Cornell economist C. Kirabo Jackson, analyzing a monetary incentive program in Texas, found the program achieved a 30% increase in the number of students obtaining high SAT and ACT scores and an 8% rise in college-going students (Jackson 2010). In addition, getting paid for grades shows the students in a tangible way what the benefits of hard work can be, much like the real world. The programs find they can get the students to challenge themselves more readily with difficult courses and learning material with the promise of a monetary award.

Ronald Fryer's study involving randomized trials at 250 urban schools (Fryer 2010) demonstrates that measurable positive results for incentives occur when the incentive is tied to the inputs to the educational process function rather than output. He argues that this is due to the fact that the incentives cannot work if the student does not know how the educational input process leads to achievement, and that understanding of the process must come first.

There are detractors to these approaches who believe they send the wrong message to students (Bodnar 2007). However, the tangible results so far are encouraging. Besides, much of their life after school will involve working for incentives anyway, namely, a paycheck.

Now that a foundation of trust and respect has been set, you can begin to nurture or re-establish the student's confidence. The keys to this are simple:

- *Be positive.* Keep an upbeat attitude, even when a student is struggling and frustrated. Assure the student that she will get past the difficulty and encourage the student to continue her efforts. This can be quite difficult at times, and some teachers give in to the temptation of doing too much of the work for the student. Do not fall into this trap. Leading questions can be posed to allow this student to get by the difficulty, and he will better remember what he did at a later time. Once a student is successful, give praise to create confidence (this is a good time for a positive parent call).

- *Have patience.* There is nothing more counterproductive when assisting frustrated students than to become a frustrated teacher. During formative learning, it is important to remember that the students are learning the material for the first time and should struggle with it a bit; naive conceptions and mistakes are normal at this point. Students will learn more from their mistakes than from their successes. Teachers must allow the students to have the time to discover the concepts and principles on their own, with the teacher providing guidance.
- *Let students catch mistakes.* One technique that has been found to be useful is to have the students correct their work in red pen when they catch a mistake as a reminder for them when they are studying for the summative assessment.
- *Make mistakes occasionally yourself.* It may sound strange, but having your students see you as human and flawed often makes them feel more confident in themselves. Praise students when they catch your error.
- *Allow the students to fail.* This may seem like a strange thing to recommend, but during formative learning, this is exactly the attitude the teacher should take, especially in early stages of learning. Taking points off for mistakes and naive conceptions at the beginning of a unit is counterproductive and can further erode student confidence. Provide the students with a safety net that allows them to explore without fear of failure. It is better to grade on effort at this stage than success. As the formative stage of learning progresses toward the conclusion, teachers can become more stringent in their requirements, but the students must have sufficient time to learn from their mistakes.

## Students Come to Class With Their Own Experiences.

A teacher puts a word problem on a white board that asks the students to calculate the work done in pulling a wagon with a mass of 3 kg for a distance of 30 m. A student timidly raises his hand and asks, "What is a wagon?"

Students bring their own experience base to the classroom, and it may diverge greatly from that of the teacher. A teacher who grew up in a rural environment of tractors and combines may struggle to formulate examples and problems for a child who grew up in the inner city. If a teacher gives an example in a lesson about forces involving a tractor to inner-city students, he may find blank faces and questions that diverge from the actual lesson. Even worse, attempts to describe what a tractor is may do nothing more than create a number of new questions about crops, tilling, and other terms students do not know.

This makes it extremely important that teachers make an effort to understand the community in which they teach and the experiences students have had in that community. Teaching examples and problems can then be formulated within that experience foundation, and misunderstandings of terminology or situation can be avoided.

If it is imperative that a student understand a concept or concepts outside their experiences, teachers must take the time to present examples or demonstrate items with which the student may not be familiar. The teacher can bring items to the classroom or use multimedia to display photographs, pictures, and movies to elicit comprehension of the new concepts. Still, this may take more time than the lesson allows. It is almost always better to formulate lessons within the existing experience foundation.

## References


Bathsheba Sculpture LLC. 2011. *www.bathsheba.com.*

Bodnar, J. 2007. Pay kids for good grades? Bad idea. *Kiplinger. www.kiplinger.com/columns/drt/archive/2007/dt071003.html#.*

Bruter, C. P. 2002. *Mathematics and art: Mathematical visualization in art and education.* New York: Springer.

Dunlap, K. 1992. *Adding it up: Math for your cosmetology career.* Clifton Park, NY: Delmar Publications (NPT).

Fauvel, J., R. Wilson, and R. Flood, eds. 2006. *Music and mathematics: From Pythagoras to fractals.* Oxford, UK: Oxford University Press.

Fryer, R. G. 2010. Financial incentives and student achievement: Evidence from randomized trials. Harvard University, Edlabs, and NBER. *www.edlabs.harvard.edu/pdf/studentincentives.pdf.*

Geist, E. 2010. The anti-anxiety curriculum: Combating math anxiety in the classroom. *Journal of Instructional Psychology* 37 (1): 24–31.

Herman, S. 2007. *Practical problems in mathematics for electricians.* 8th ed. Florence, KY: Cengage Learning.

Jackson, C. 2010. A little now for a lot later: A look at a Texas Advanced Placement incentive program. *Journal of Human Resources* 45 (3): 591–639.

Kaplan, K. *Los Angeles Times.* 2010. Female teachers may pass on math anxiety to girls, study finds. January 26.

Keeley, P. 2008. 10 key points about formative assessment. Formative Assessment. *http://science-assessment.wikispaces.com/Formative+Assessment.*

Keeley, P., F. Eberle, and C. Dorsey. 2008. *Uncovering student ideas in science, volume 3: Another 25 formative assessment probes.* Arlington, VA: NSTA Press.

Keeley, P., F. Eberle, and L. Farrin. 2005. *Uncovering student ideas in science, volume 1: 25 formative assessment probes.* Arlington, VA: NSTA Press.

Keeley, P., F. Eberle, and J. Tugel. 2007. *Uncovering student ideas in science, volume 2: 25 more formative assessment probes.* Arlington, VA: NSTA Press.

Moore, E. 2008. *PHCC plumbing 301.* 3rd ed. Falls Church, VA: Plumbing-Heating-Cooling Contractors Association.

Ohio Math Work. 2000. Fashion: Fabrics and formulas. Ohio Math Work. *www.ohiomathworks.org/fashion/f_fashion.htm.*

Smith, L. 2007. *Mathematics for plumbers and pipefitters.* Florence, KY: Cengage Learning.

Sparks, S. 2011. Researchers probe causes of math anxiety. *Education Week 30 (31): 1–16.*

Tarko, V. 2006. Money incentives can prop up the brain to remember things. *Softpedia,* May 5. *http://news.softpedia.com/newsPDF/Money-Incentives-Can-Prop-Up-the-Brain-to-Remember-Things-22816.pdf.*

Tobias, S. 1995. *Overcoming math anxiety.* New York: W. W. Norton.

Toppo, G. *USA Today.* 2008. Good grades pay off literally; controversial program offers cash incentives. January 28. 3A.

Webster, A. P., and K. B. Judy. 2001. *Mathematics for carpentry and the construction.* Upper Saddle River, NJ: Prentice Hall.

# CHAPTER 3

# Yes, Virginia, Study Habits and Learning Techniques Are Key!

## The Importance of Lower-Order Thinking Skills: Memorization

Teachers like to point out in discussions pertaining to higher-order thinking that their students often struggle with lower-order thinking. Their point is well taken. There has been a trend away from making students memorize material. For example, the advent of the calculator has perpetrated a trend away from memorizing multiplication tables in many schools. The big question becomes the following: How can we expect a student to memorize complicated problem-solving processes if they can't even memorize simple lists of names or facts?

In the endeavor to push the attainment of higher-order thinking skills in students, educators often forget that the lower-order skills provide the foundation. It is important that students be re-engaged with tasks that require memorization, such as memorizing multiplication tables or state capitals, especially in early learning to set the stage for learning the higher-order skills later.

Teachers can assist students in mastering these lower-order skills by giving them memory tools such as mnemonics. As an example, consider these two mnemonics: "FACE" and "Every Good Boy Deserves Fudge." The first one gives the notes on the spaces of a music staff, and the second gives the notes on the lines of the music staff. Lists of useful mnemonics for mathematics and science may be found in a variety of sources (Math Mnemonics; Mnemonic Devices). Mnemonics are just one example of a variety of systems available for assisting memorization of materials that include word mnemonics, number mnemonics, rhyme mnemonics, shape mnemonics, link methods, story methods, alphabet techniques, roman room systems, major systems, and journey systems. Presentations and examples of each of these important memorization aids can be found in a variety of sources (Jones 1995; *Mind Tools* 1996).

In addition to the memory techniques listed above, teachers can improve memory by remembering three keys:

- Make sure that all sensory modalities are engaged. Engaging sight, sound, and even touch can make the learned information more real for the student. Laboratories and multimedia are good sources for this kind of teaching.
- Try to make the information interesting, relevant, or useful to the student. Research suggests that when information has one or more of these attributes, students will remember what they have learned more easily.
- Find ways to link the information with information already integrated into a student's memory. This technique actively models how information is integrated into memory, thus accelerating the integration.

The responsibility for developing memorization skills in students lies squarely with elementary and junior high school teachers. The younger the student is when developing and practicing these skills, the better they are able to master and use them later. However, memorization skills can be improved at any age, and teachers in later grades need to work memorization tasks into their curriculum, especially for students who may have missed out on them in earlier grades. Again, success in developing higher-order thinking skills is fundamentally linked with mastery of these lower-order thinking skills.

## Why Taking Notes Is Important

In this age of emphasis on student-centered learning, educators sometimes forget to consider skills that are required for success in the traditional classroom. Students often demonstrate deficiencies in note-taking, even in upper-level courses.

Why is good note-taking an important learning skill?

- *The student becomes active in the process of learning and listening.* Simply listening to a lecture or presentation is rarely effective in eliciting comprehension and can lead to boredom and off-task behavior.
- *The student develops a history and synopsis of the course content.* Through the notes, the student has a ready synopsis of the lessons that can delineate the overall structure and development of the subject.
- *The student has information necessary for preparation for assessments.* The notes provide a foundation for study and review that is more targeted than a textbook alone.
- *The student reinforces what is communicated verbally and in writing.* The notes provide a structured recording of the lessons that assists the transfer of the lesson from teacher to student.

In addition, being able to take notes accurately and efficiently is a critical skill for success in a college classroom, where the traditional teacher-centered approach often still dominates.

Students must be capable of summarizing the presentation given by an instructor with sufficient detail and accuracy and in real time. Most students have to learn this skill; it is not something that they can do without practice. Learning the skill in secondary school is important because the pace of material presentation accelerates in college. If the student cannot record the information at a sufficient pace with adequate accuracy, it can adversely affect the successful completion of a degree.

Secondary teachers should integrate enough traditional teaching into their lessons to allow the mastery of the note-taking skills. Grading the notebooks periodically is a good way to get students to take the skill seriously.

Muskingum College has provided a comprehensive presentation of note-taking strategies and techniques that teachers may review for insight. The website also contains a comprehensive overview of learning strategies in a wide variety of topics (Muskingum 2011). The particular note-taking topics covered in this book have been found to be particularly effective.

## *Cornell Notes*

One particularly effective method of note-taking is called Cornell Notes (Pauk 2001), which was developed by education professor Walter Pauk at Cornell University for the purpose of improving student mastery and retention of course material. The system is designed to take note-taking beyond the passive recording of presented material to an active tool for promoting student comprehension and memorization of the subject material.

See Figure 3.1 (p. 36), which illustrates how a page is divided into three sections for taking Cornell notes. Section 1 is for the recording of presented material—the information that comes from lectures, demonstrations, or audiovisual material. Section 2 allows for quick summarization of points in the material by the student and the expression of questions pertaining to information recorded in Section 1 that the student may have (answers can be recorded here also). Finally, Section 3 provides an area for the student to summarize what he or she learned.

The goal of Cornell notes is to elicit active thinking by the student during note-taking rather than the often passive recording of traditional outlining techniques. By making the student formulate questions about the material, the student goes beyond the simple recording of words or pictures and must think about the inherent meaning. Furthermore, the summary deepens this consideration by the student by urging them to put their understanding of the material in his or her own words. If the teacher demands a succinct summary, the students are forced to get to the heart of what they have learned.

## FIGURE 3.1

Cornell Notes Page Layout

| ← 2 1/2 inches → | ← 6 inches → |
|---|---|
| **Cue Column**<br>**Questions and Cue words:** As soon after a class finishes as possible, formulate questions and cue words based on the notes in the right-hand column. Formulating questions helps to clarify definitions, relationships, and processes. This also strengthens memory of the material.<br>**Recite:** Cover the note-taking column with a sheet of paper. Then, looking at the questions or cue words in the question and cue column only, say aloud, in your own words, the answers to the questions, facts, or ideas indicated by the questions or cue words. | **Note-Taking Column**<br><br>**Record:** During the lecture, use the note-taking column to record the lecture or other presentation material. Notes from active reading and observation of multimedia material can also be recorded in this column.<br><br>**Reflect:** Reflect on the material by asking yourself questions, for example: "What's the significance of these facts? What principle are they based on? How can I apply them? How do they fit in with what I already know? What's beyond them? |

**Summary**
After class, summarize the notes in this box.

**Review:** Spend at least 10 minutes every week reviewing all your previous notes. If you do, you'll retain a great deal for current use, as well as for the exam.

*Adapted from PAUK/OWENS. How to Study in College 10E. ISBN 9781439084465 © 2011 Wadsworth, a part of Cengage Learning, Inc. Reproduced by permission. *www.cengage.com/permissions*

It should be noted that this technique is not limited to science and mathematics and has been found to be effective for note-taking in a wide variety of courses. Students should be encouraged to use it in the entirety of their classroom note-taking efforts.

A student-produced example of Cornell notes is given in Figure 3.2 (p. 38).

### *Interactive Notebooks*

A modern method for executing active note-taking is the interactive notebook (Bower, Lobdell, and Swenson 1999), a system developed for note-taking and the exhibition of understanding of the material by the student. This technique has been found to enhance learning because it conforms to modern brain-based learning research (Blakemore and Frith 2005; Underwood 2006). For the student to execute an interactive notebook, the following materials are necessary:

- 8.5 × 11 in. bound notebook with at least 100 pages of lined paper
- Glue stick
- Colored pens
- Crayons or colored pencils
- 3 different color highlighters

Interactive notebooks have been successfully incorporated by many teachers in a variety of subjects. The notebooks have become an integral part of the success of the AVID program (AVID 2006), whose goal is to prepare at-risk students displaying academic potential for entry into challenging college programs.

Each notebook has a cover, a page for grades to be recorded, a page for the grading rubric, and several pages for a table of contents, where titles and page numbers are recorded for each note page. The remaining pages are designated for notes and activities, with the right-hand pages specifically designated for input given to the student (class notes, video notes, notes from reading) and the left-hand pages used specifically for student output (written descriptions, problem solving, drawings, concept maps, and any other demonstration of student understanding of the material). See Table 3.1 (p. 39) for a complete description of the interactive notebook.

The notes on the right-hand page should use the Cornell notes format as described previously (see Figure 3.1).

The key to effective use of the interactive notebook system is creativity on the left-hand pages. Students should be encouraged to highlight vocabulary in colors, make colored drawings to demonstrate a concept or principle, paste in articles and pictures they find that demonstrate concepts and principles, paste in foldable constructions that demonstrate understanding, and so on. Anything is allowed as long as it directly addresses the learning objectives as outlined on the right-hand pages. The creativity aspect promotes engagement in the learning tasks not available using traditional note-

## FIGURE 3.2

Student Example of Cornell Notes

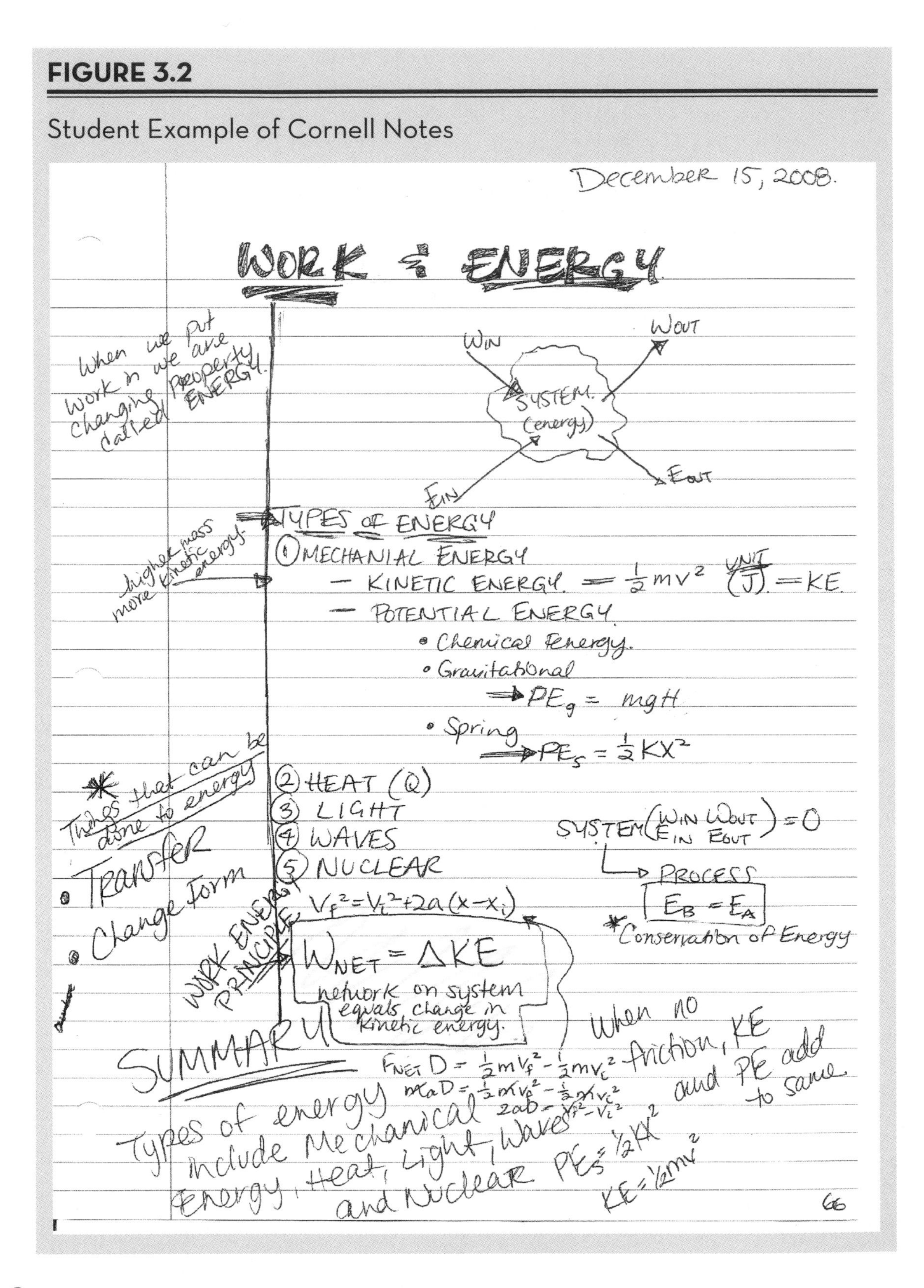

**TABLE 3.1**

Overview for an Interactive Notebook

| Left Side<br>Students Process New Ideas | Right Side<br>Teacher Provides New Information |
|---|---|
| • Reorganize new information in creative formats<br>• Express opinions and feelings<br>• Explore new ideas | • Class notes<br>• Discussion notes<br>• Reading notes<br>• Handouts with new information |

Materials Needed: colored pencils and markers, scissors, glue stick, rulers, etc.

| Left-Hand Side | Right-Hand Side |
|---|---|
| The left side of the notebook (the "output" side) is primarily used for processing new ideas. Students work out an understanding of new material by using illustrations, diagrams, flow charts, poetry, colors, matrices, cartoons, etc. Students explore their opinions and clarify their values on controversial issues, wonder about "what if" hypothetical situations, and ask questions about new ideas. They also express their feelings and reactions to activities that tap into intrapersonal learning. And they review what they have learned and preview what they will be learning. By doing so, students are encouraged to see how individual lessons fit into the larger context of a unit.<br><br>The left side of the notebook:<br><br>• Stresses that writing down lecture notes does not mean students have learned the information. They must actively do something with the information before they internalize it.<br>• Clearly indicates which ideas are the teacher's and which are the student's. Everything on the left side is student ideas and belongs to the student.<br>• Gives students permission to be playful and experimental since they know the left side is their page and they will not be interfering with class notes.<br>• Allows students to use various learning styles to process social studies information. | The right side of the notebook (the "input" side) is used for recording class notes, discussion notes, and reading notes. Typically, all "testable" information is found here. Historical information can be organized in the form of traditional outline notes. However, the right side of the notebook is also an excellent place for the teacher to model how to think graphically by using illustrated outlines, flow charts, annotated slides, T-charts, and other graphic organizers. Handouts with new information also go on the right side.<br><br>The right side of the notebook:<br><br>• Is where the teacher organizes a common set of information that all students must know.<br>• Gives students the "essentials" of the social studies content.<br>• Provides the teacher with an opportunity to model for students how to think graphically. There are many visual ways to organize historical information that enhance understanding. |

*Courtesy of Laurie Swigart

**FIGURE 3.3**

Student Example of an Interactive Notebook

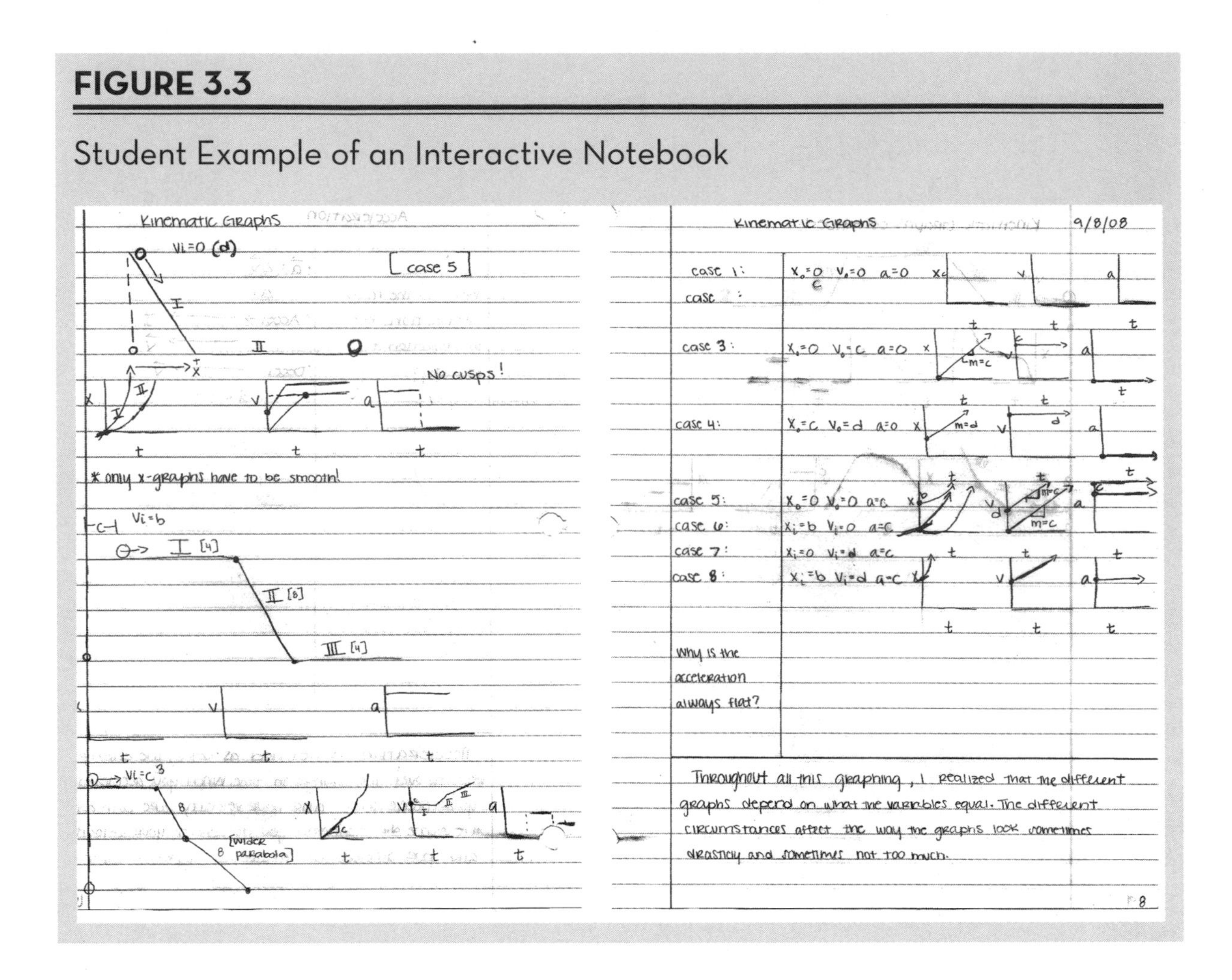


taking techniques. Appendix B provides a rubric for grading an interactive notebook. Figure 3.3 displays a student example of pages from an interactive notebook.

### *Note-Taking and Listening*

No matter what technologies a student uses to take notes, and no matter the techniques, the student needs to be able to do more than copy information. The student must be able to record fast enough to keep up with the presentation of information and have enough time to listen. Listening is often lost in the rush to record, but it is just as important to learning and comprehension.

Accelerating the rate of note-taking can be a daunting task, especially when the presentation of material is being done by electronic means. In addition, the rate at which information is presented becomes greater as students enter a collegiate environment. Couple this with the fact that many students have difficulty writing legibly, and the challenge becomes clear.

In the face of these challenges, what strategies can a student use? Here are some recommendations:

- *Use outlines and/or concept maps.* Sometimes students try to write down every word, written or spoken, from the teacher. This is unnecessary. By creating outlines or concept maps, a student can capture the information in a more compact form.
- *Use shorthand.* Students should be encouraged to develop their own system of shorthand to replace words in their notes. For example, you can use a double-lined arrow for what the word implies or abbreviations for longer words.
- *Use recording technologies.* Use tape recorders or computer recording technologies during lecture presentations. This allows the student to listen better and concentrate on diagrams and other nonverbal information. Students may be able to use video recording and capture the entire presentation, although there is the danger that the student's mind will wander for lack of activity. Note that the student may need to ask permission of the teacher to execute recording of material.
- *Get the notes from the teacher.* Acquiring complete or guided partial notes from the teacher can provide the student with significantly more time to listen and comprehend presented information. Guided notes, where the student has opportunities to enter information into blanks in the notes, are especially effective because they prompt the student's thinking and help them maintain concentration and focus.

## Rewriting Notes

When I first began my own collegiate experience, I often struggled with studying for tests and quizzes, especially tests covering large amounts of material taught over a significant period of time. I felt overwhelmed with the sheer quantity of material and limited time to prepare. The result was less-than-efficient studying for the assessments. My grades were decent, but I knew they could have been better.

A professor recommended that I change my philosophy and approach to studying by rewriting my notes from classes soon after the class in which the notes were composed. He suggested that the act of rewriting and re-organizing my notes was a better study technique and would result in better understanding and recall. He was right.

My grades improved significantly, and the amount of time necessary to do the final preparations for tests and quizzes was drastically reduced. In fact, I found that the extra time I spent rewriting the notes allowed me to be more efficient and, ultimately, saved time. In addition, my confidence level during the assessment was significantly better, allowing for better concentration and less trepidation.

The key to the effectiveness of rewriting notes is that the process of rewriting the notes is more than preparation of study material; the process actually helps integrate the material into the knowledge base of the student.

Here are some suggestions for students to execute the rewriting of their notes:

- Rewrite notes the same day they are taken in class. Maximum efficiency and benefit will occur when the course material is fresh in the mind. It also keeps the student from falling behind the class schedule and losing the benefit of time management.
- Organize the rewritten notes in a logical structure using outline format or graphic organizers—whatever format best fits the student's learning style. Matching notes to learning style and improving the organization of the material improves the learning aspect of the process and provides better notes for assessment preparation.
- Use library resources and reputable websites to fill in information that was unclear during the initial taking of notes in class. Using resources to improve the notes by research further enhances the learning aspect of the rewriting process. This is one of the most important steps in the process, as it clears up naive conceptions well before the assessment and further integrates the knowledge into the student's synaptic map. Note that it is important to use reputable resources in the process. Employing the websites of well-known universities and institutes for the research is a good way to make sure the information is of good quality.

It is important for teachers to get parents to buy into this process, as students will rarely execute rewriting notes on their own. Initially, students see the rewriting process as extra work and often fail to understand the nature of the benefits until they have experienced them for themselves. Having parents direct the early efforts is key to attaining student buy-in to the process.

## *The Note Collage*

Computers, both desktops and laptops, have become prevalent in the modern student's life. Much is made of the effects this technology has on students, both good and bad. Many teachers, fearful of the technology and news reports of abuses surrounding computers and the internet, shy away from integrating computers into their lesson planning. However, the technology isn't going away, and it behooves educators to find positive ways to apply the technology to improve the education process. Many states and school districts are forcing the issue by investing in computerized education technology, with mandates concerning its use in the classroom.

Given the new hardware placed in my own classroom (each student has desktop access and a wireless tablet computer), I directed my effort to ascertaining the best and most efficient way to integrate the technology into the learning process. This effort has lead to a new method of note rewriting that takes full advantage of the strengths of the technology. This method is called a note collage, a method of rewriting notes that integrates full multimedia and active simulation into the rewritten notes.

All of the rules for note rewriting are still applied for a note collage, but the following must also be followed:

- The student must use a word-processing program for the note rewrite that has automated content tables, an equation editor, and the ability to insert hyperlinks into the text. This will allow equations and information from the internet to be inserted into the notes. Microsoft Word and Corel WordPerfect both have these attributes. If graphic organizers better fit the student's preferred learning style, online graphic organizer software such as Cmap or Inspiration may be used (discussed in a later section of the book). The Microsoft program OneNote is an excellent tool for note-taking if students have access to tablet PCs. The program interfaces easily with all other Microsoft programs in the Microsoft Office suite and provides a flexible interface for forming and organizing notes for a note collage. It has the capability to take typed information or handwritten input with a stylus and includes character recognition to convert handwritten text to printed text.
- The note collage must be formed as a single document with numbered and dated pages. The note collage should begin with an unnumbered title page, rubric page (provided by the teacher), and automated table of contents. Each page of the note collage after the table of contents should have a heading, followed by the note content. The headings become part of the automated table of contents. The purpose of these attributes of the note collage is to make finding information in the notes quick and easy during study for assessments.
- In addition to the text-based outlines or graphic organizers of typical note rewrites presented in the last section, documents, graphics, photos, movies, and simulations from the internet are linked into the documents. These links become part of the outline or graphical organizer structure. This is the strength of the note collage. Paper notes are limited in that they can only present static information. But a note collage, composed and used on the computer, is dynamic and interactive. Graphics and photographs from paper media and the internet can be printed and pasted into paper notes, but formulating the notes on the computer allows movies and simulations to be included. Movies provide a better way to study and understand any time-dependent phenomenon as the time dependence can be observed explicitly by the student.
- Even more important to effective learning is the ability to integrate links to simulations and applets into the notes. These interactive programs (often freely available from a variety of reputable sources) allow the student, individually or as part of a group, to actively explore concepts and principles through manipulation of parameters and observation of the resulting simulation response. This activity provides an efficient and inexpensive supplement to laboratory work for the exploration of new concepts and principles as the simulations and applets mimic real laboratory phenomena. These simulations and applets can be found by internet search for almost any topic from a variety of reputable sources. Many universities and some research institutes and companies have large banks of them

that can be accessed for free as long as they are not used for commercial gain. In contrast, some companies provide access to simulations for a fee. Note that in some cases, use of the simulation or applet will require the download of supplementary software.

Teachers should assess students' note collages to provide incentive to the students to do an adequate job on them while learning the process. Teachers should encourage students to record the learned skills and knowledge gained from viewing movies and manipulating simulations and applets into the note collage near the associated link. This enforces effective learning from the dynamic media. Often, the simulations and applets are accompanied by lessons and questions to direct student learning. Teachers need to encourage students to work through these lessons.

### *Keeping an Equation Sheet*

In addition to keeping good notes, students should be encouraged to keep an equation sheet (or card) on which each equation is written as it is introduced in the course. Each equation should be written in standard form, and each variable in the equation should be defined. This equation sheet (or card) can be used by the student during problem solving to keep the student focused on the process of solution instead of the search for an equation. It will also allow the student to re-examine and apply equations at later stages of the course as they re-appear in the context of other learning units.

## Studying for Tests

I once asked a student who had failed a test how he had studied for it. His response was surprising and enlightening: "I read over my notes."

Typical tests in mathematics and physical science involve three types of questions. The first pertains to understanding concepts through definition and behavior. The other two types of problems involve problem solving and laboratory questions for science courses. The problem-solving questions ordinarily comprise the largest part of the points on an exam.

It often surprises teachers that students do not understand that these types of courses require a different type of study than other courses. Problem solving, whether mathematical or conceptual, is the true key to mastery and needs to be the focus of preparation for summative assessment. A student who can solve any problem pertaining to the principles of a given unit has truly demonstrated mastery. It means that the student understands the structure of the principle and concepts, can recognize the applicability of the principle in a given problem, can apply the principle in generally applicable situations, and has mitigated any naive conceptions about the concepts and principles that often occur during learning.

Students must realize that in general they are not being asked to memorize facts, but to understand principles and be able to apply these principles. In other words, students need to place reasoning above factual knowledge. Indeed, recent research into the effect of learned factual science knowledge on science reasoning suggests that there is little or no effect (Gorder 2009). The study compared reasoning skills of students in China, where there is significantly more knowledge of science facts, with U.S. students, where there was significantly less knowledge of science facts. Contrary to recent thinking, there was no perceptible difference in reasoning abilities between the two sets of students.

Students sometimes become angry when the same problems they had worked during their learning are not on the test. This demonstrates a common misunderstanding that often occurs when students don't comprehend the purpose of their learning in a course of this type. Teachers must make sure the students understand they are expected to know the principles and procedures necessary to solve any problem of a given type. It isn't about memorization of facts, but understanding of principles and memorization of processes. It isn't about solving a given problem, but the process necessary to solve a class of problems.

Students attain this kind of mastery one way: by working enough problems that they comprehend the pattern of processes and the application of principles necessary for all problems of that type.

## Maps on Paper = Maps in the Head

The effectiveness of graphic organizers as teaching tools lies in two attributes. The first has to do with connecting with students whose visual intelligence exceeds their printed word or mathematical-logical intelligence. This encompasses a fairly large percentage of students. Indeed, researchers have found pictorial representations to be superior in eliciting memorization in most students and that they are preferred by 80% of students in surveys (Chanlin 1997; June and Huay 2003; Nooriafshar and Maraseni 2005). Even for those students who prefer textual or symbolic presentation of material, the use of graphic organizers, along with the text or symbolic representations, can enhance their understanding.

The second attribute has to do with the close connection with how the brain stores knowledge by integrating the new knowledge within a pre-existing synaptic map of previously learned concepts. The new knowledge is integrated into the old map through a rewiring of the synapses and connections to related concepts within the map. Graphic organizers can mimic this map and thus aid in the rewiring process.

Graphic organizers come in different styles, and teachers often develop styles to meet their own needs and teaching methods (e.g., bubbl.us, Cmap, Inspiration, Make Sense Strategies, Mindmeister, Thinking Maps):

- *Thinking Maps:* This collection of eight maps is designed to mimic common thought processes to elicit higher-order thinking skills (*www.thinkingmaps.com*). They may be used separately or combined to model more complex representations and processes. Thinking Maps, Inc., provides documentation on their usage in the classroom and professional development for the teacher. Figure 3.4 displays the eight maps.
- *Make Sense Strategies:* An extensive collection of graphic organizer templates are available at *www.graphicorganizers.com* and may be downloaded for free.
- *Inspiration:* A software package that produces colorful and highly visual graphic organizers (*www.inspiration.com/Inspiration*), Inspiration is also capable of translating a graphic organizer directly into an outline. There are more than 120 templates available in the software package for a variety of subjects. This is an excellent choice for the artistic students in a class. Figure 3.5 (p. 48) displays a graphic organizer for the laws of motion, as produced using Inspiration.
- *bubbl.us:* A free online tool for creating colorful graphic organizers that may be printed, e-mailed, saved as an image, or mounted in blogs or websites (*http://bubbl.us*)
- *Mindmeister:* An online and collaborative tool for creating graphic organizers. A limited version can be downloaded for free for evaluation (*www.mindmeister.com*).
- *Cmap:* Cmap is a powerful online tool for creating graphic organizers that takes full advantage of online capabilities (*http://cmap.ihmc.us/conceptmap.html*). Created by the Institute for Human and Machine Cognition (IHMC), Cmap is a free tool that creates graphic organizers that may be linked to documents, multimedia, websites, and other graphic organizers online, even those created by other users. This software is especially useful for forming note collages in a graphical manner. Figure 3.6 (p. 49) displays a Cmap graphic organizer for the properties of water created by NASA as part of a large set of linked maps for Mars exploration.

Regardless of the tools used to produce the graphic organizers, here are recommendations for increasing the effectiveness of graphic organizers:

- *Keep the organizer as simple and clear as possible.* Graphic organizers should enhance learning and memory, not inhibit them. Organizers with too many nodes and branches, or too many crossing connectors, can act as a deterrent to learning by overwhelming the student's ability to comprehend the implied pattern. One good approach to simplification is to make smaller graphic organizers with links between them. This is particularly easy to do with Cmap software.

**FIGURE 3.4**

Thinking Maps

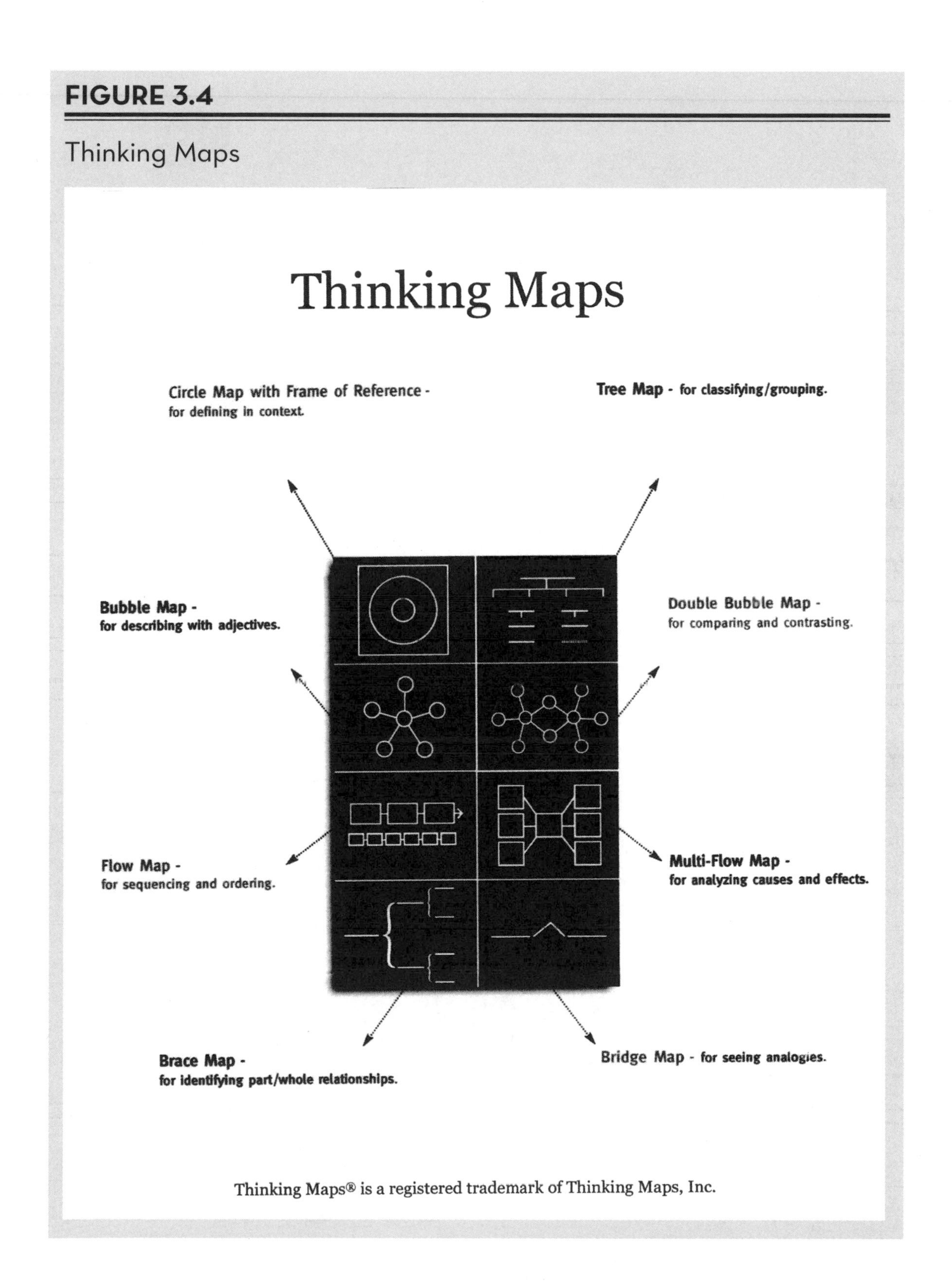

**FIGURE 3.5**

A Graphic Organizer: Laws of Motion Inspiration

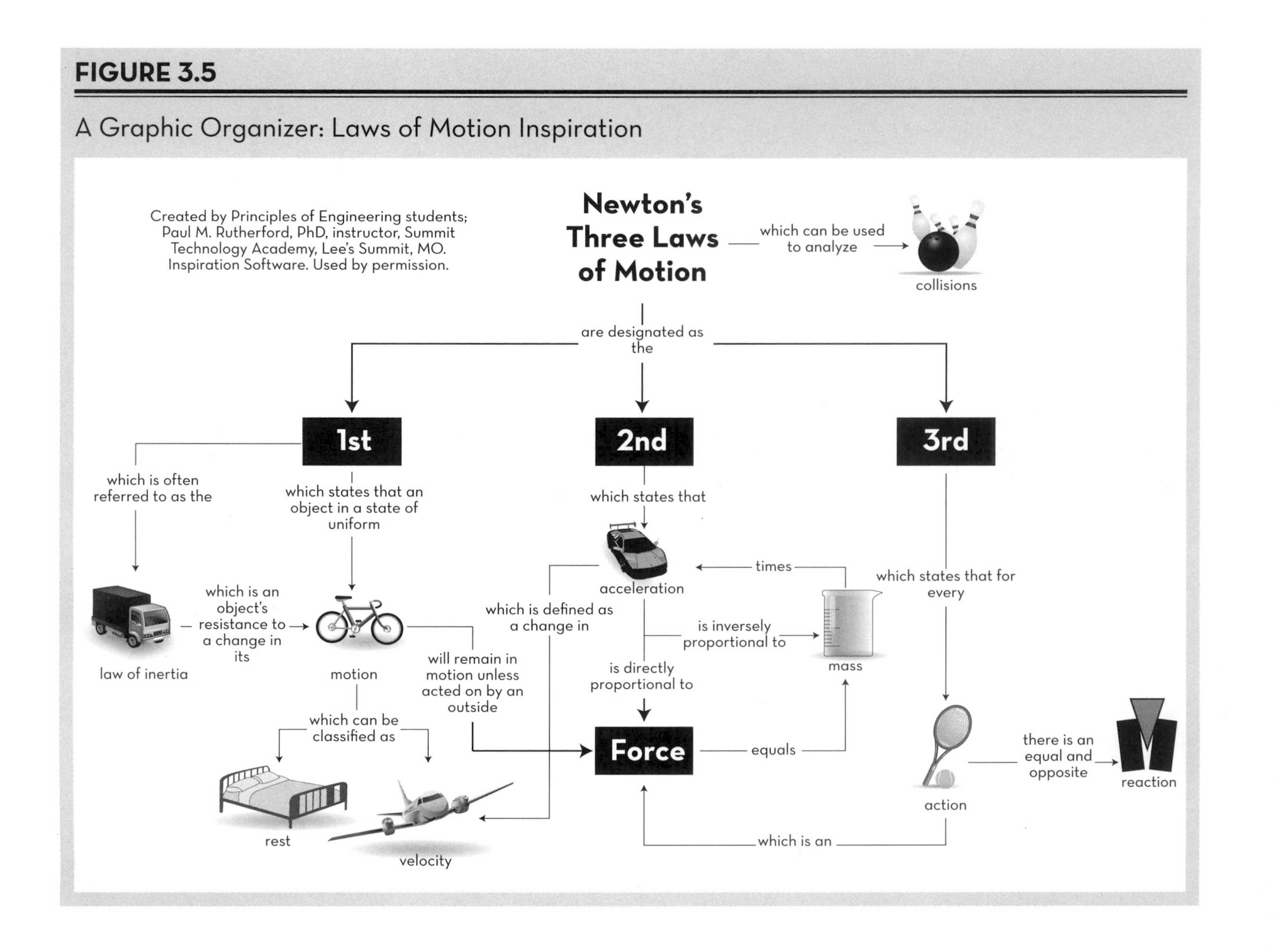

**FIGURE 3.6**

NASA Graphic Organizer Cmap

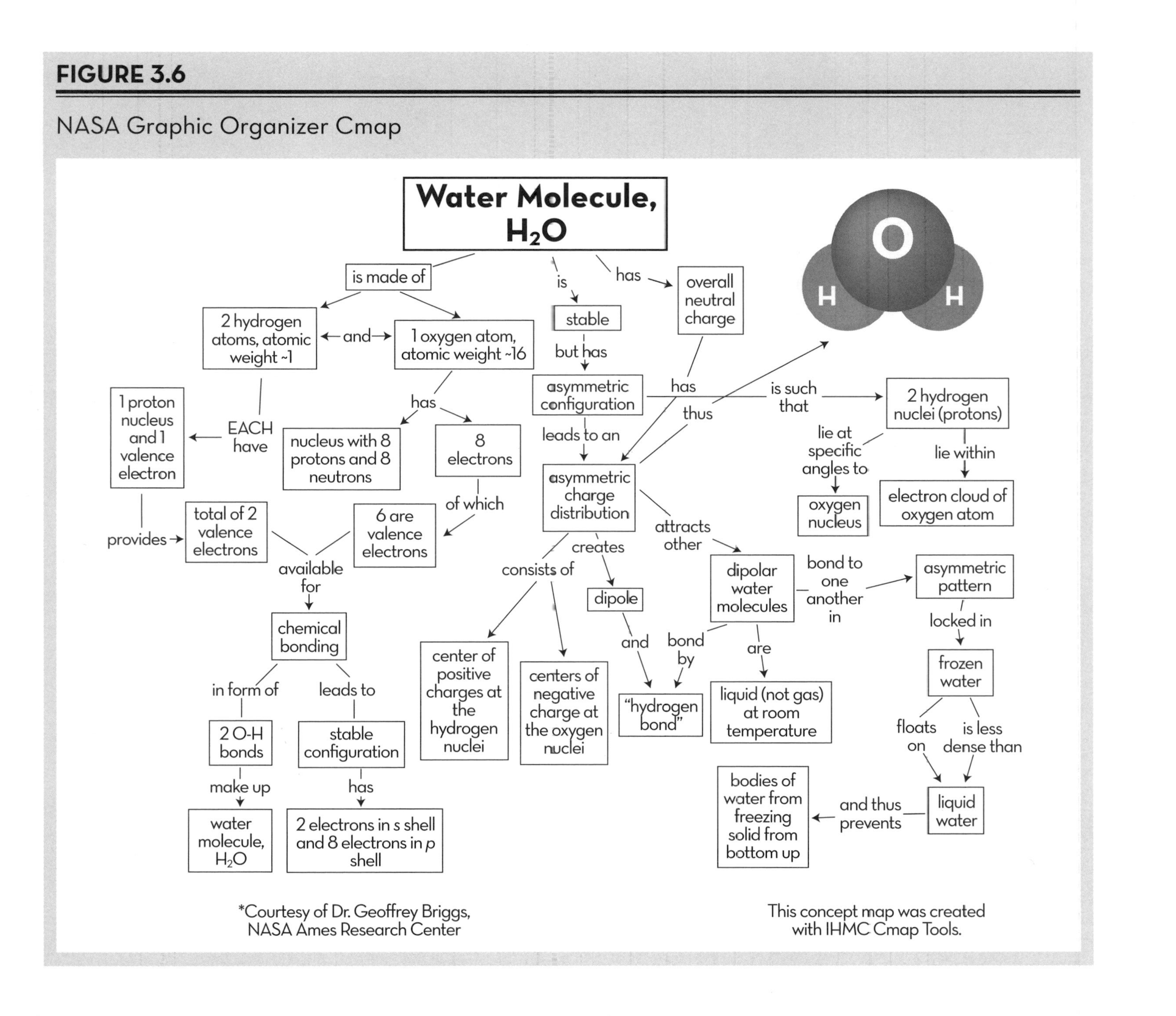


*Courtesy of Dr. Geoffrey Briggs, NASA Ames Research Center

- *Organize your organizers.* Oftentimes, organizers for a subject can be made to follow a standardized pattern that can be repeated for each new introduced concept. For example, when introd cing physical concepts, you might always have a bubble for units, a bubble for a word definition, a bubble for an equation, and a bubble for naive conceptions. As students become comfortable with the standardized format used, they will find it easier to understand and integrate the map into their own synaptic maps.
- *Map concepts, rules, laws, and processes.* Having an organizer or set of organizers that can handle all of the types of information or processes that a teacher might introduce is useful. Thinking Maps are a good foundation for formulation of organizers to handle logical processes and attributes in the learned material. These maps provide a set of representational tools that model various logical processes in learning, such as attributes, similarities and differences, processes, and categorization.
- *Make direct connections to previously learned concepts within the maps.* By making these connections explicit, the teacher helps the student form the new connections with their internal synaptic map.
- *Make students formulate their own maps.* Once a teacher has made their students comfortable with a style of organizer, it will enhance learning and memory if the students can formulate their own maps for the subject material.

Figure 3.7 displays a student example of a graphic organizer.

## Less Homework, More Class Work!

Homework is the source of much consternation among teachers and disagreements among researchers and policy makers (Buell 2009; Center for Public Education 2007; Keates 2007; Penn State 2005; Penn State 2007; Sharp, Keys, and Benefield 2001). Students' failure to do or complete homework is a common complaint among teachers. For some reason, many teachers place great stock in the effectiveness of homework in learning, and assign hours of problems and questions for after-school time. Ironically, though, this work is rarely given that much weight in computing grades compared to tests, quizzes, labs, reports, or projects. Without the incentives, students often put little time into the homework. In addition, much of the homework is given a simple completion grade, as the teachers find they cannot possibly grade it all for correctness or review entire assignments with today's modern class sizes and time constraints.

The disagreement between research studies on the correlation of homework hours and achievement is almost contentious, with some studies showing benefits and others pointing toward comparisons with schools from different nations that seem to suggest little or anti-correlation between more homework hours and achievement. The problem comes down to the number of variables that can influence how effective homework is in the learning process. Here are some of these factors:

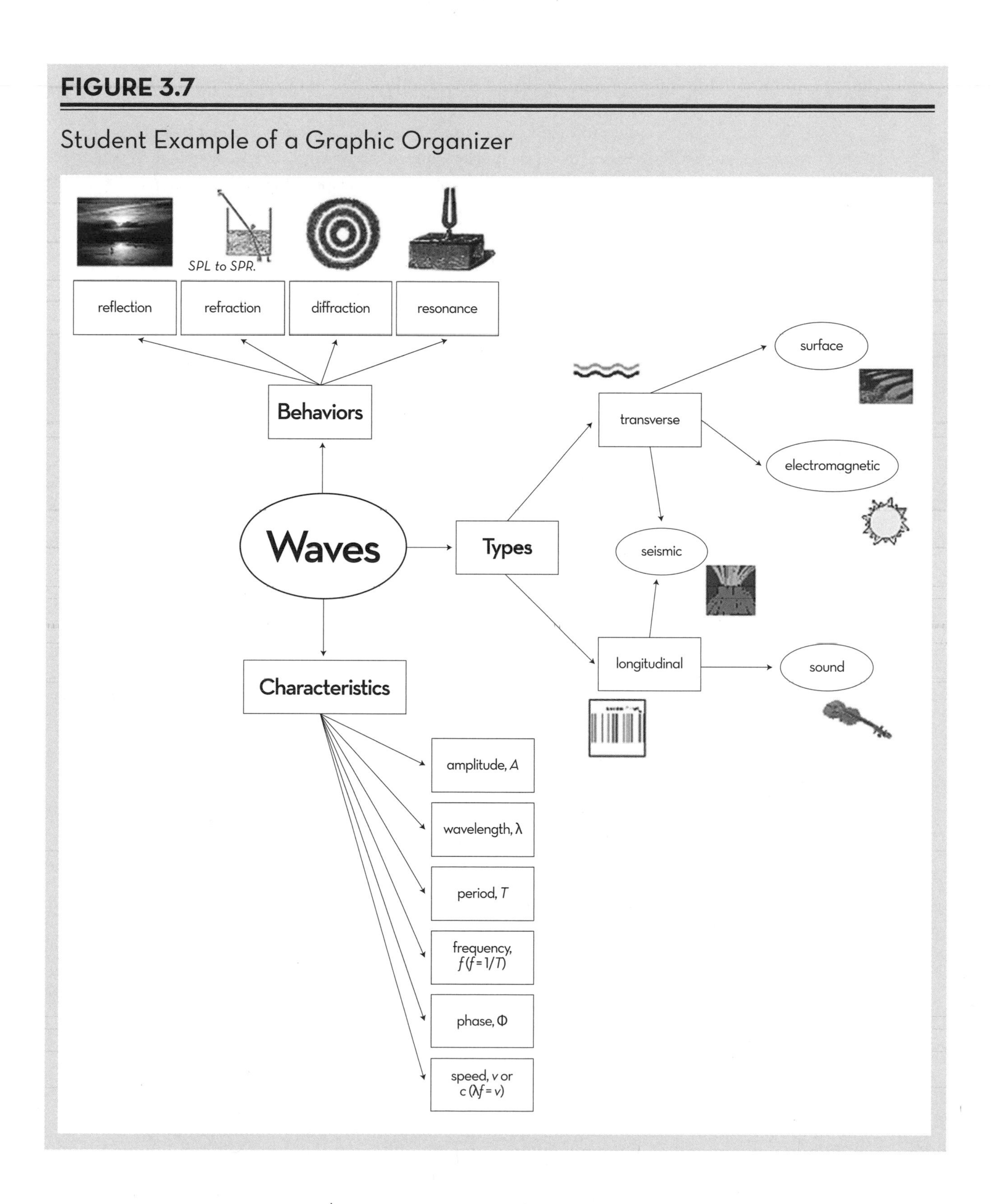


**FIGURE 3.7**

Student Example of a Graphic Organizer

- *Age of the student:* Younger students require less time with homework while older students require more. Studies show positive effect of homework on secondary school students, while the studies for primary school students are, in general, inconclusive. The experts recommend two hours of homework for grades 6–9 and two and a half hours of homework for grades 10–12. Despite this, some students are performing four hours or more of homework per night, leading to little time for relaxation and other activities, boredom, and loss of necessary sleep time.
- *Home environment:* The quality of the home environment can affect a student's ability to benefit from homework. This can include amount of distraction, support from parents, and availability of help. These factors can vary widely over a group of students, with teachers having little control over the situation except to make recommendations to the parents.
- *Graded versus ungraded:* Research clearly shows that students take homework much more seriously if it is graded. However, as stated earlier, grading a large amount of homework is often impossible with the larger class sizes and new responsibilities of the modern classroom.
- *Focusing curriculum:* Many experts suggest that the real problem comes down to focusing the curriculum. For example, U.S. textbooks often cover many more topics than comparative textbooks in other nations. This lack of focus often causes a need for more homework to cover the broad set of objectives. These experts recommend that the curriculum and resulting homework be focused on a smaller set of learning objectives.

With other factors such as course type, student gender, and socioeconomics also showing some influence on the effect of homework on the learning process, it is not hard to see why there is so much disagreement.

So the question is, What real benefit comes from assigning large amounts of homework to students? Let's examine some practical arguments against homework:

- *Homework places time stress on students.* U.S. students spend an average of four hours per night on homework assignments. The stress of this much homework can inhibit learning by taking any fun out of the process, especially if it inhibits a student's ability to participate in leisure activities. Drudgery is not an ally to effective learning; it is the enemy. It is important that children have time to be children and participate in activities that can make them well-rounded individuals.
- *Homework is rarely effective in learning, but is effective in solidifying mastery.* Without the dynamic feedback, many students struggle to complete challenging homework assignments in the home environment. In many cases, parents lack the knowledge and abilities to assist the student on difficult assignments. This

struggle can lead to frustration and a sense of failure in students. Homework is better geared for practice toward final mastery rather than initial learning of the subject matter.
- *Homework for completion grades is merely busywork.* If homework is not adequate for learning and isn't being assessed, what exactly is its purpose? The answer is often that there is no real purpose except late-stage practice for mastery before summative assessments.

So, what should be done about homework? It is not being suggested here to eliminate homework completely, but rather to simply decrease the amount and focus on a smaller set of objectives. Here are some suggestions that have been found to be effective in formulating and assigning homework:

- *Replace as much of the homework with classwork as possible.* Providing class time to tackle difficult assignments allows the teacher to dynamically monitor a student's progress and stem any naive conceptions (using active observation and formative assessment probes) that may arise during the process. This is in contrast with homework, which is often unmonitored and ungraded. Unfinished classwork is assigned as homework for completion.
- *Provide the students with three- to four-week homework schedules.* Giving the students a calendar of their assignments well in advance of the due dates allows the student to plan a schedule better and prevents homework from piling up before due dates.
- *Keep homework short and to the point.* Longer homework assignments rarely have added value in learning. Questions and problems should be chosen to attack the specifics of what the teacher is focusing on and what should be graded and reviewed. Two problems for each objective or skill are plenty if the student is also tackling similar problems in the classroom environment.
- *Save homework time for projects, papers, and reports.* There is no choice for these types of assignments other than being produced, in whole or in part, at home. These types of assignments often require substantial time to be prepared adequately. The time necessary for these types of assignments should not be robbed from the schedule by simple question or problem assignments.
- *Save homework for mastery rather than initial learning.* Homework is a good way to get practice just before a summative assessment. Use it in that context, not for initial learning.

## Don't Throw Away Anything!

Have you ever examined the folder of a typical student? I remember examining a student's folder where all of the returned assignments and handouts were crumpled into balls and stuffed into pockets. Of course, this is a worst-case scenario; however, it is not atypical to find students who throw out their handouts and assignments, even when there is a final exam looming at the end of the course or semester. Even when all the materials are kept, students often place them in the notebook haphazardly, making use of them for later study difficult.

Teachers must make students aware of the importance of keeping assignments and handouts in an orderly folder and encourage them to do so. Like their notebooks, these folders will become increasingly important to their success in later academic pursuits, especially in college or trade school programs.

Some suggestions with regard to these folders can be made:

- *Fasten the sheets, no pockets.* There is a reason the words *loose* and *lose* sound so much alike. Teachers should discourage students from placing sheets in pockets and encourage the use of folders with rings or other types of fasteners to keep the paper in place and in order. Reinforcements are an excellent tool to make sure handouts and returned assignments do not tear out of the binder over time.
- *Have students place handouts and returned materials in a folder by date or topic.* Keeping the material in a logical order will allow the material to be accessed more efficiently during study activities at a later date, especially when reviewing for a final or semester exam.
- *Grade the binder.* Like the notebook, students sometimes require an incentive to keep a well-ordered binder. Giving a grade can do that. Giving this grade once every six weeks should be adequate for this purpose.

## Safety in Numbers: Group Work

The advantages of cooperative learning (group work) as a learning technique are undeniable. Studies of its effectiveness are well documented (Slavin 1992; Susman 1998; Ziegler 1981), but the best practices on how it is implemented have changed over time. Unlike whole-class instruction, which is often about competition, group work requires cooperation. This cooperation is the key to its effectiveness, as all members of the group bring their individual strengths and ideas to the group.

There is much to be said for using as much group work as possible in teaching, but there are also pitfalls that must be avoided. Some of the obvious benefits of group work are the following:

- *Students are exposed to a collaborative environment, much like the one they will be exposed to in the workplace.* Students learn to handle the psychology and dynamic of working with people who have different ideas and work habits.
- *Students in a group environment become answerable to the group, thus enhancing responsibility.* Placing students in an environment that encourages responsibility prepares them for the rigors of later adult work environments.
- *Group work gets to the heart of student-centered learning.* The group lessons allow for greater student autonomy and self-exploration while providing a forum for the exchange and debate of ideas. Teachers act as facilitators and monitors in this environment.
- *Group work is effective in learning.* Research has proven that group work is more effective in student comprehension and retention of subject matter than traditional whole-group lecture instruction.

Even with these significant benefits, getting the most out of group activities requires vigilance on the part of the teacher in the identification and mitigation of potential problems. Some potential problems that could surface include the following:

- *Students drift.* Sometimes the purpose of the work may be misunderstood by the group or lost in their discussions and activities. The group may go off on tangents that are far afield of the learning objective of the task. The teacher, acting as a facilitator, can prompt the group back on task by asking leading questions that help the group focus. Here are some examples of possible leading questions:

    - What is the relationship implied by your data table (or graph)? Can you write the relationship as an equation?
    - What numbers can you extract from your graph?
    - What model do you think explains the phenomenon you are observing and why?
    - What systematic errors in your experiment did you observe? How could you eliminate or lessen them?
    - Where in your experience have you observed a phenomenon like this? How is it related to your experiment?

- *Students accept roles within the group.* It is human nature to gravitate to roles that fit your comfort zone. Some students gravitate toward leadership, others toward active follower, and still others toward passive roles. There will always be those students who attempt to slide by and let others in the group produce the learning product. It is imperative that teachers observe the working groups and discourage this tendency. To be truly effective, all students within a group must be forced to participate to the fullest extent and stretch outside their comfort zone. This applies as much to the leader types as to slacker types.

The approach to cooperative learning taken 20 years ago involved having the teacher assign the roles and then change the roles often to make sure everyone was working, being exposed to all aspects of collaborative work, and learning. This has changed because this approach was found to be ineffective in keeping all members of a group engaged at all times and did not guarantee that all group members learned the target material at the same level. The most recent research encourages the teacher to have all of the individuals in the group fully engaged with all tasks. There are two ways in particular that students can become disengaged from their groups or the whole group can become dysfunctional:

- *Group becomes a social club.* This is probably the most common problem that arises. Teachers must work hard to keep the groups focused and on task. Challenging these groups to produce a hard product within the class period can force this issue when prompting fails. In addition, the teacher should monitor and challenge groups with questions about their activities as they are conducted to keep the groups on task.
- *Social friction in a group.* Every group dynamic has the potential for friction among the participants. It is human nature. It might seem that the teacher should try to separate students who can't get along and redefine groups of students that result in a minimum of arguing; however, real-life group work does not have this luxury, and students need to learn to cope with different personalities and viewpoints. Instead of avoiding conflicts, the teacher should arbitrate disagreements and teach students methods for dealing with this natural dynamic as part of their education. Patience, sensitivity, and humor are the teacher's best tools for working with groups suffering from social dysfunction. Make sure that the group's attention is directed toward the task and away from personality conflicts by using leading questions to elicit constructive conservation and promote quality progress toward a product.

In math and science classes, cooperative learning often revolves around problem-solving activities or laboratory investigations, but group work can be used throughout a learning unit. A recent book by Dr. Bertie Kingore stressed the importance of using diverse groupings for group instruction as a way to meet the diverse instructional needs of students (Kingore 2004). Table 3.2 displays each of the four types of groupings, their advantages and disadvantages, and the type of instruction for which they are best suited.

Given the strengths of each of the grouping types, there is a logical order of application of the groups to the stages of instruction for a learning unit:

## TABLE 3.2

### Diverse Groupings for Instruction

| Grouping Type | Advantages | Disadvantages | Application |
|---|---|---|---|
| Whole-class instruction | • Students learn to interact with everyone in the class.<br>• Less labor-intensive and more effective for initial presentation of the lesson material | • Students tend to be less engaged.<br>• Pace and level of instruction may not be optimal for all students. | • Introduction of material for a learning unit<br>• Assessment reviews<br>• Project presentations<br>• Class discussions<br>• Final review discussions |
| Mixed-readiness small groups | • Modeling of real-world work environment<br>• Diverse ideas<br>• Students tutoring fellow students<br>• Perception of equal expectations | • Learning groups geared to the middle of the group's capability levels, which limits effectiveness for advanced and struggling students<br>• Some students tend to take too much or too little responsibility for the tasks. | • Student tutoring of fellow students<br>• Initial practice activities<br>• Real-world social interaction activities<br>• Laboratory activities |
| Similar-readiness small groups | • Pacing and complexity of material can be uniform for all members of a group.<br>• Comfort of learners | • Lack of role models for less-skilled students<br>• Danger of labeling the capability of the students | • Advanced practice activities<br>• Extension of knowledge for advanced students<br>• Focused remediation for struggling students |
| Individual work | • Matching of students' paces, levels, and interests<br>• Individual responses to questions for pre-assessment<br>• Preparation for assessments | • Less-motivated learners tend to get off task.<br>• Students become isolated; lacks social interaction<br>• Labor-intensive for teacher | • Assessment preparation<br>• Practice for mastery<br>• Elaboration |

Note: Adapted from Kingore, B. 2004. *Differentiation: Simplified, realistic, and effective.* Austin, TX: Professional Associates Publishing.

- *Introduce the material with whole-group instruction.* The beginning of any unit requires that the teacher disseminate a certain amount of basic material to the class. Lecture and whole-class activities are the most efficient ways to place this basic information in front of all the students. Teachers must make sure that students are engaged and active during this type of instruction. Using a mixture of leading questions and short, student-centered activities helps greatly with this.
- *Use tutoring, initial practice, and laboratory work with mixed-readiness groupings.* Humbling as it may be to teachers, sometimes students learn best with assistance from their fellow students. Forming groups with a good mixture of skill levels allows the upper-level students to assist struggling students. Many of the highly skilled students find it rewarding to help their fellow students, and having the students help allows the teacher to move more quickly from group to group for monitoring and assistance. This type of grouping is particularly effective for laboratory work, as it results in a good mixture of opinion and approaches to the work; however, teachers must carefully monitor the lab activities to make sure all members of the group are active and engaged in the work.

  It is not recommended that mixed-readiness groupings be used for all practice work for a unit. One disadvantage of this type of grouping is that it tends to concentrate on the middle of the group's capabilities. Highly capable students eventually become bored if they are not challenged, and struggling students can become lost.
- *Achieve mastery of the material through similar readiness groupings.* Once a basic level of skill is acquired by all the students, it is most efficient to place students in similar readiness groupings to work toward mastery. These groupings allow students to work with the same materials and advance at a rate similar to their fellow group members without the risk of anyone getting intimidated or bored. Teachers should be cautioned that this type of grouping can be the most challenging to monitor. Students from groups that are struggling will try to monopolize the teacher's time or get off task, while highly skilled students will need advanced material to extend their mastery.
- *Use whole-class instruction for assessment reviews.* Reviewing for an assessment is most efficiently accomplished through whole-class instruction. This process allows students to benefit from questions asked by their fellow students and the answers given by the teacher. Again, teachers must use a series of probing questions and short activities to guarantee student engagement during this kind of instruction.
- *Incorporate individual work for assessment preparation.* Students do not generally take assessments in groups. Therefore, individual work must constitute the last stage of instruction before the assessment to guarantee students are ready for

the exam. During this practice, teachers should walk around the classroom, monitoring engagement and offering assistance when students are struggling.

Here are some suggestions to teachers for implementing cooperative learning in their classes:

- Make all students in a group responsible for the same deliverables individually. This discourages the tendency for one or two group members to produce most of the work and keeps all individuals of the group engaged. The group as a whole needs to guarantee that every member of the group produces a good product through discussions and assistance. All members of the group should be able to answer probing questions posed by the teacher.
- Grading should be done on individual and group aspects of the work. Each individual should get a grade for his or her own work, with a separate grade given for the group responsibility of making sure all members have produced and learned (swim or sink together). This grading approach makes sure the cooperative aspects of group work are encouraged. Group members need to understand up front that they are all responsible for that aspect of their grade. This understanding discourages off-task behavior and personality conflicts.
- Group membership should be dynamic, changing as needed within the Kingore diverse groupings model and class needs (circumventing personality conflicts, for instance). The teacher must work hard to monitor the work of each group and be conscious of potential conflicts among group members. One tactic that is effective in cases of conflict is to pose a question and make both parties responsible for the answer. Again, the goal is to encourage cooperation.
- Make safety the responsibility of all group members. All group members should be aware of potential safety threats and be able to state the mitigation strategies formulated by the group.

There are many excellent books on group work and cooperative learning. The books by Johnson, Johnson, and Holubec (1994) and Kagan (1994) are highly recommended. The key to group work is to encourage a cooperative mentality and approach to the work (all sink or swim together) while making sure that each individual contributes and takes responsibility for a significant deliverable. Every member of the group is made responsible for the learning of all members. These books provide the research basis for cooperative learning, tools to encourage cooperation, cooperative learning activities, and strategies teachers can use in the classroom to foster successful group work.

# CHAPTER 3

## The Digital Child

Susie wakes up to a world of digital technology. This world contains televisions, home computers, laptop computers, mobile phones with cameras and internet, video games (consoles and handhelds), high-definition televisions (HDTV), digital recorders, and handheld digital music and movies. She is bombarded by multimedia from a variety of sources and participates in blogging, wikis, podcasts, and social networking. Everything in her world reaches her in color, motion, and sound, fast and furious. She chooses what she sees and when, often changing from one source to another at a whim. So, how can a teacher standing in front of a whiteboard with a marker compete with that?

The truth is, he can't, unless he is willing to embrace the technology himself and integrate it into his lessons. Students are no longer the passive listeners of the past, and they require active roles in the learning environment. The good news is that school districts and media providers are embracing the challenge and have created and implemented a wide variety of targeted technologies to address the needs of education and educators. These technologies include digital whiteboards, laptop and tablet computers, multimedia libraries, online tutoring and homework services, streaming video, online textbooks, digital probeware, virtual laboratories, simulations, and many other aids to deliver content to students.

The sheer variety of the offerings can be daunting to any teacher. The key to navigating the choices is to match the technologies to the nature of the lesson content by trial and experimentation and to modify and adapt the technologies over time to increase the efficiency and effectiveness of the technology in the specific course. Not all technologies will be right for your particular course content or teaching style, while others will be too expensive or impractical for your particular situation.

For example, dynamics problems in physics where there are moving objects are best served by video media rather than still media because the dynamic nature of these problems can be best visualized by moving media. Simulations and virtual laboratories are even more effective as learning tools as they provide for active manipulation and experimentation by the student, which allows them to ask questions and be actively engaged.

Take advantage of any expertise in the school district or from reputable online and off-line sources when making technology decisions and planning the use of technology in instruction. This should include participation in a multitude of professional development opportunities. In addition, your fellow teachers, who have already integrated technology into their teaching, can often be the best resource in your own planning, and many will be happy to assist you in the effort.

There isn't enough room in this book to talk about all the issues that must be addressed in teaching the digital child. However, it is important that teachers make an effort to keep abreast of new offerings, issues, and ideas, many of which will be advertised in education periodicals, professional development sessions, or presented at education conferences. Changing and modifying technologies used in your classroom will keep the students excited and engaged with the technology-assisted lessons, while ensuring that the students don't become bored with them.

In addition, it is crucial that teachers work toward balance so their teaching doesn't become more about the technology than about course content. Stepping back from the technology regularly and using low-tech approaches, such as class discussions and paper-and-pencil group work, is advised to keep this balance and ensure that students don't become jaded about the technology.

Finally, patience and diligence are necessary for effective integration of technology in the classroom. In the course of technology integration, not all ideas will work as planned, and significant time may be needed to address issues and execute changes. Teachers need to understand this, stay positive, and be flexible in adjusting their approach.

## All Hail the 5E Learning Cycle!

Constructivist models of education have been found to be extremely effective in the learning process. These models allow the student to discover, comprehend, and apply concepts and principles, rather than getting them directly from textbooks. By having students discover the concepts and principles and develop their own understanding of them, learning and retention are enhanced. Several constructivist learning cycle models have been proposed, but the current one used in many schools, with good results, is the BSCS 5E learning cycle (Boddy, Watson, and Aubusson 2003; Bybee et. al. 2006; CSCOPE 2007).

The 5E learning cycle is composed of five parts:

1. *Engagement:* A question is posed or a demonstration is presented to the students to elicit discussion on the concepts and principles of the lesson. The teacher provides motivation and enthusiasm. Engagement makes initial connections between these new concepts and principles and the student's prior knowledge. In science, a demonstration involving new concepts and principles is most effective for eliciting these connections. In math, the teacher may propose an application that requires the new concept or principle and ask the students how they would approach the application.
2. *Exploration:* The student uses laboratory investigations and simulations to discover the properties of the new concepts and principles for themselves. The teacher acts as a facilitator and guide. Students develop their own comprehension of the lesson. The discussion of laboratory work that will be presented in Chapter 8 is based on this approach.
3. *Explanation:* The student communicates his or her understanding of the new concepts and principles. The teacher provides guidance and clarification and promotes discussion. This is where understanding is refined and naive conceptions are discovered and mitigated. In science, student presentations, formative assessments (formative assessment probes presented in Chapter 2), and laboratory discussions provide a check on the understanding gained in the exploration step.

4. *Elaboration/Extension:* The student applies the new concepts and principles, extends the learned material to new applications and topics, and uses new terminology. The teacher provides guidance and encourages new learning based on the previously learned material. In science and mathematics, this is where problem solving becomes important. True understanding of concepts and principles requires that the student be able to apply them to real-world application problems. This is where the subtleties of the subject matter and hidden naive conceptions may be discovered and mitigated. A systematic method for problem solving will be discussed in Chapter 5. This method has been found to have a positive effect on the efficiency and success of student problem solving.
5. *Evaluation:* The student's understanding of the concepts and principles is assessed. The teacher assesses student knowledge and skills and encourages students to assess their own learning. These assessments may take the form of traditional paper tests, laboratory or project reports, oral assessment, or portfolio activities that can be evaluated by the teacher. Teachers can also use the results of these assessments to modify and refine their lessons.

Figure 3.8 displays an excellent example of a 5E lesson plan developed by a participant in the E3 Program, a National Science Foundation Research Experience for Teachers project at Texas A&M University.

## FIGURE 3.8

### Example of a 5E Lesson

**Unit Topic:** Chemical reactions
**Note:** This lesson may take two days to complete.
**Title of Lesson:** Water Resources Engineering
**Class:** Chemistry
**Student Objectives:** The student will be able to

1. evaluate the impact of research on scientific thought, society, and the environment.
2. describe the connection between chemistry and future careers.
3. identify oxidation-reduction processes.
4. demonstrate and explain effects of temperature and solute material properties on the solubility of solids.
5. develop general rules for solubility through investigations with aqueous solutions.
6. evaluate the significance of water as a solvent in living organisms and in the environment.
7. describe effects of acids and bases on an ecological system.

#### Materials

- Soil Profile handout
- Enough of the following materials for each student: clear plastic cups, spoons, Rice Krispies treats, M&M's, peanut butter, crushed chocolate graham crackers, shredded coconut
- Overhead/computer
- Transparencies/PowerPoint presentation

## FIGURE 3.8 *(continued)*

I. Engagement: This should puzzle and motivate students in an activity or lesson.

☺ You will need a focus activity/question to engage students in the task/assignment at hand.

**Focus Questions**

What is engineering? (general)

What is water resources engineering? (specific)

II. Exploration: This should allow students to explore today's topics.

☺ You will need a task/assignment/lab that allows student to work individually or in small groups with little or no help from the instructor.

**Soil Profile Activity**

*Students work individually.*

*The students will receive handouts to build their own soil profiles.*

*Allow 2 or 3 min. to read and explain the handout prior to starting the profile and 7–9 min. to complete the profile.*

III. Explanation: This allows for focusing/narrowing in on today's objectives.

☺ Have students present/discuss their observations of the topic.

**Class Discussion**

*What observations did students make? Discuss as a class.*

*Key point during discussion should be observation made when colored water was trickled down the profile.*

*For instance, on what layer did the colored water seem to stop? Why?*

Answer: *Students should have noticed that the colored water seemed to stop trickling down once it got to the peanut butter representative of the B horizon. The B horizon—combined with the O, A, and E horizons—makes up a region of the soil known as the solum, which means true soil. The B horizon is the Zone of Accumulation, where chemicals leached out of the topsoil accumulate. It is has a higher content of clay (particle size 0.002 mm). Furthermore, most of the roots of the plants grow in the solum.*

*Write down (as a class) the different crops that are grown in the Rio Grande Valley.*

*Corn, sugarcane, carrots, palm trees, cabbage, onions, oranges, watermelons, etc.*

*Use sugarcane as the prime example since the excel spreadsheet uses sugarcane as the example.*

*Key Point: Valley agriculture is important to the economy. Transition into Water Resources Planning Engineering.*

☺ Teacher narrows in on objectives:

Factual info (mainly from Background Information):

*Discuss the importance of water to crops. How do we determine the amount of irrigation supplied according to amount of rainfall?*

*What happens if there is a lot of rain or not enough? The amount of water is critical to the crop yield.*

*Chemistry: What happens when farmers supply sufficient water but harvest a poor quality crop? Insufficient plant nutrients may be the issue.*

IV. Elaboration: Allow students to comprehend and apply the information.

☺ You will need a homework, worksheet, etc. to assign.

*Example lesson courtesy of Enrichment

**Homework**

Experiences in Engineering

*Ion and Solubility Rules/Oxidation Number worksheets* (E3) Program at Texas A&M University.

**Closure**

*What do you think about engineering now?*

V. Evaluate: Allow students to demonstrate knowledge and comprehension of objectives.

☺ Plan for a future test/quiz over these objectives.

*Solubility Rules*

*Oxidation Numbers*

The challenge of implementing the 5E model often lies in time management. It takes time to incorporate the entire cycle, and this often runs contrary to the required scope and sequence of a course and the actual number of classroom days in a year. Teachers must use judgment in the implementation, determining how much time that can be allocated for each part of the cycle. New teachers should acquire guidance and suggestions from experienced teachers and attend professional development courses pertaining to the 5E learning cycle. It is also recommended that teachers reflect on their first implementations of the cycle so that efficiencies and improvements may be found for the next time the 5E cycle is executed.

## The Joy of Modeling Instruction

Modeling Instruction adds structured knowledge to the 5E learning cycle by organizing course content around a small number of scientific models, thus making the course coherent (Hestenes 1987, 1997, 2006; Jackson, Dukerich, and Hestenes 2008; Megowan-Romanowicz, 2010a, 2010b, 2011; Wells, Hestenes, and Swackhamer 1995). Students are taught from the beginning that modeling is a central activity of scientists, engineers, and businesspeople, and that "the game of physics is to develop and validate models of physical phenomena" (Hestenes 1992, p. 740). In two- to three-week modeling cycles, students engage collaboratively in building scientific models, evaluating the models, and applying them in concrete situations. A modeling cycle has these two stages:

*Stage 1:* Model development begins with description. A demonstration of some physical phenomenon is followed by a guided class discussion that prompts students to identify some fundamental relationship to explore (e.g., the relationship between force and acceleration in a modified Atwood's machine; the relationship between pulling force and length for a stretched spring). Then students, in small groups, plan and execute a laboratory investigation to uncover the relationship. Afterward, each group writes their findings on large (24 × 32 in.) whiteboards, using multiple representations for the data they have collected. Then, the class gathers as a whole group for a "board meeting," during which students examine each others' representations and interpretations of their data and make sense of the general model for the relationship they have uncovered. The teacher acts as a discourse manager, facilitator, and guide. Terminology and tools are suggested by the teacher as needed to refine the models and stimulate discussions. The teacher is aware of typical naive conceptions that can occur for the phenomenon in question and uses this knowledge to guide classroom discourse in ways that will assist the students in the development of their models.

*Stage 2:* In the model deployment stage, the students test the boundaries of the model by using it to solve progressively more challenging problems and make reasonable predictions when engaging in real-world lab practices. These activities are again done in small groups and discussed as a class using representations on whiteboards prepared by the individual groups. Formative assessment tasks are used frequently throughout the course of each instructional unit to assess the coherence of students' conceptual models as they develop. Paper-and-pencil testing and occasionally lab practicum assessments are administered at the end of the unit to summatively assess students' final understanding.

An example of the application of the Modeling Instruction cycle is given in Figure 3.9 (courtesy of J. Jackson, C. Megowan-Romanowicz, and L. Dukerich of Arizona State University). It is recommended that teachers become familiar with the reference articles mentioned above.

Modeling Instruction is a highly effective pedagogy (Expert Panel Reviews 2001, 2000). However, it is a very different design for the learning environment from traditional science courses you may have experienced. For this reason, the Modeling Instruction Program strongly recommends that teachers attend a three-week workshop before attempting a full implementation of modeling pedagogy. Workshops are offered at universities and in school districts across the country each summer. (Visit *http://modeling.asu.edu* to locate a workshop near you.)

Note that just as with the 5E cycle, there may be time-management challenges with the scope and sequence of the course that must be taken into account by the teacher while he or she learns to use Modeling Instruction. As with the 5E cycle, professional development, experienced guidance, and active reflection are recommended.

## FIGURE 3.9

### Example of a Modeling Instruction Lesson

#### Modeling Cycle Example: The Constant Velocity Model

**I. Model development**

*Prelab discussion:* The teacher demonstrates battery-powered vehicles moving across the floor and asks students to make observations. Students suggest possible influences on the motion and eventually agree on the most important variables. Then each group of three or four students designs a laboratory investigation to describe the vehicle's motion and relate the variables.

*Lab investigation:* Each group collects position and time data for a vehicle, from which they generate a graph by hand or use data-collection technology. From the graph, they develop an equation. On a 2 ft. × 2.5 ft. whiteboard, they specify their system (the vehicle modeled as a point particle) and describe their model with diagrammatic, verbal, graphical, and algebraic representations. In this case, the diagrammatic representation is a motion map, the graph of position versus time is linear, and the slope is the average velocity.

## FIGURE 3.9 *(continued)*

*Postlab discussion:* Groups refer to their whiteboards as they present and justify their conclusions to the class, including a formulation of their model of the vehicle's motion and evaluation of their model by comparison with data. The teacher introduces technical terms and concepts as needed to sharpen the descriptive model of constant-velocity motion and improve the quality of discourse. Student lab notebooks and lab reports emphasize model development.

**II. Model deployment**

*Worksheets and formative assessment:* Working in small groups, students complete practice problems by applying the constant-velocity model to new situations. They write their solution strategies on a whiteboard, using multiple representations and appealing to the model developed on the basis of experiment. The teacher listens and guides the whole-class discourse, more by questioning than by telling. The teacher presses for explicit articulation of students' thinking, often by asking, "Why do you say that?" and "How do you know that?" to address lingering naive conceptions. Formative assessment includes quizzes, which students complete individually to demonstrate their understanding of the model and its application. Students must explain their problem-solving strategies.

*Lab practicum:* As a culminating activity that helps students review key principles for the unit test, the class completes a lab practicum using the constant-velocity model to solve a real-world problem. Students test their solution with battery-powered vehicles.

*Unit test:* As a final check for understanding, students take a unit test. The constant-velocity unit is the first unit. In later units, students develop causal particle models that incorporate models developed earlier; this is an example of the spiral nature of Modeling Instruction.

## Wow! There Is a Reason They Taught Me Algebra!

When students are exposed to chemistry and physics classes, they often realize why they were required to learn algebra and geometry. Mathematics in these science classes becomes less about formal manipulation and more about application. The variable names that students have become comfortable with in their mathematics classes ($x$ and $y$, for instance) are replaced with variable names or combinations that fit the concepts introduced. The unfamiliar variable names can make it harder for some students to recognize equation types and patterns. This poses a challenge to the science teachers to assist the students in seeing the patterns they know from their mathematics classes in algebraic expressions containing these new variables.

One recommendation to mathematics teachers is that these types of variable names and combinations be introduced during the mathematics classes so students become accustomed to seeing them earlier, before they take the actual science classes. This will allow students to become comfortable with these variables while learning the manipulation rules. This goal is best accomplished by collaboration between science and mathematics teachers.

### *Math and Science Teachers Should Be Partners.*

It is not uncommon for the science and mathematics staffs at a school or in a school district to work in isolation from each other, rarely sharing techniques, knowledge, or materials. This is an unfortunate state. The two fields share a common foundation and purpose, albeit with different emphasis: Mathematics teachers concentrate on the teaching of rules, concepts, and manipulation skills, while science teachers emphasize mathematics application. Given this close relationship, why do the two entities insist on working and planning apart?

This problem often seems to start at the district level, with science and mathematics coordinators caught up in political haggling. It is crucial that district superintendents encourage coordinators and department heads in science and mathematics to work together closely on curriculum so that the needs of both subjects are met.

### *Strengthening the Mathematical Foundation*

The most common complaint heard from upper-level science and mathematics teachers is that their students arrive at their courses with inadequate prerequisite mathematics skills. We have already discussed how this can be mitigated, but precious time could be saved if we could figure out how to avoid the problem in the first place.

To improve the comprehension and retention of math skills, teachers need to work together on strategies that reinforce learned material. Science teachers can be a great help to math teachers by reinforcing the use of mathematics rules in the performance of work in their class, thus pushing the knowledge and skills deeper into long-term memory. Science teachers can also assist the mathematics teachers in the formulation of practical word problems that allow the student to get experience in applying the calculation skills they are learning before they take the science class.

Mathematics teachers can also be a big help to science teachers. Collaboration between the two departments would allow the mathematics teachers to know what skills are vital to science and need to be stressed in the lesson planning. In addition, the collaboration would allow the joint production of preassessments for prior knowledge as discussed earlier.

## STUDENTS CAN BUILD CALCULATION AND ANALYTICAL SKILLS (DESPITE THEMSELVES).

### *Reaching for Higher-Order Thinking*

As students prepare for the rigors of college, it is important that they have the ability to think at a high level, performing creative, analytical, and evaluative skills at the top end of Bloom's taxonomy (Bloom 1956; Forehand 2005; Krathwohl 2002) as part of the collegiate courses. These skills are developed through a process of hands-on investigation and elaboration (encompassed by the 5E cycle and modeling instruction discussed earlier) that builds them from the student's knowledge foundation. Figure 3.10 (p. 69) displays the typical skills and processes a scientist might perform in a course of study. Teachers need to develop the sophistication of these skills in the students by providing incrementally more sophisticated tasks for the students to perform. In this way, the students have these skills in place before handling the rigors of college course work.

Teachers need to keep in mind that students will develop these skills at varying paces and levels of difficulty. Flexibility, encouragement, and patience are the keys to success with this type of teaching.

### *The First Step in Many Directions*

Even if the student has no intention of pursuing a career in mathematics, science, medicine, or engineering, the skills developed in mathematics and science courses are closely linked to skills that are helpful in any professional environment. Evaluative, creative, and analytical thinking are as applicable to business as they are to engineering or science. Algebraic manipulation is universal, appearing in many professions.

It is important that teachers in science and mathematics use tactics that elicit critical thinking and creativity to develop these skills for later execution. It is often helpful to talk to the students who are not in pursuit of technical careers about the big-picture view of these higher-order thinking skills so they have a broader appreciation of the importance of mathematics and science education for their future.

### *The Importance of the Foundation: Lower-Order Thinking Skills*

As stated earlier, the lower-order thinking foundation should not be ignored. The best approach integrates the development and refinement of both lower-order and higher-order skill development in the student. Students who start college with these integrated skills in place have an excellent foundation for success in their college curriculum and subsequent career.

**FIGURE 3.10**

Research Scientific Processes

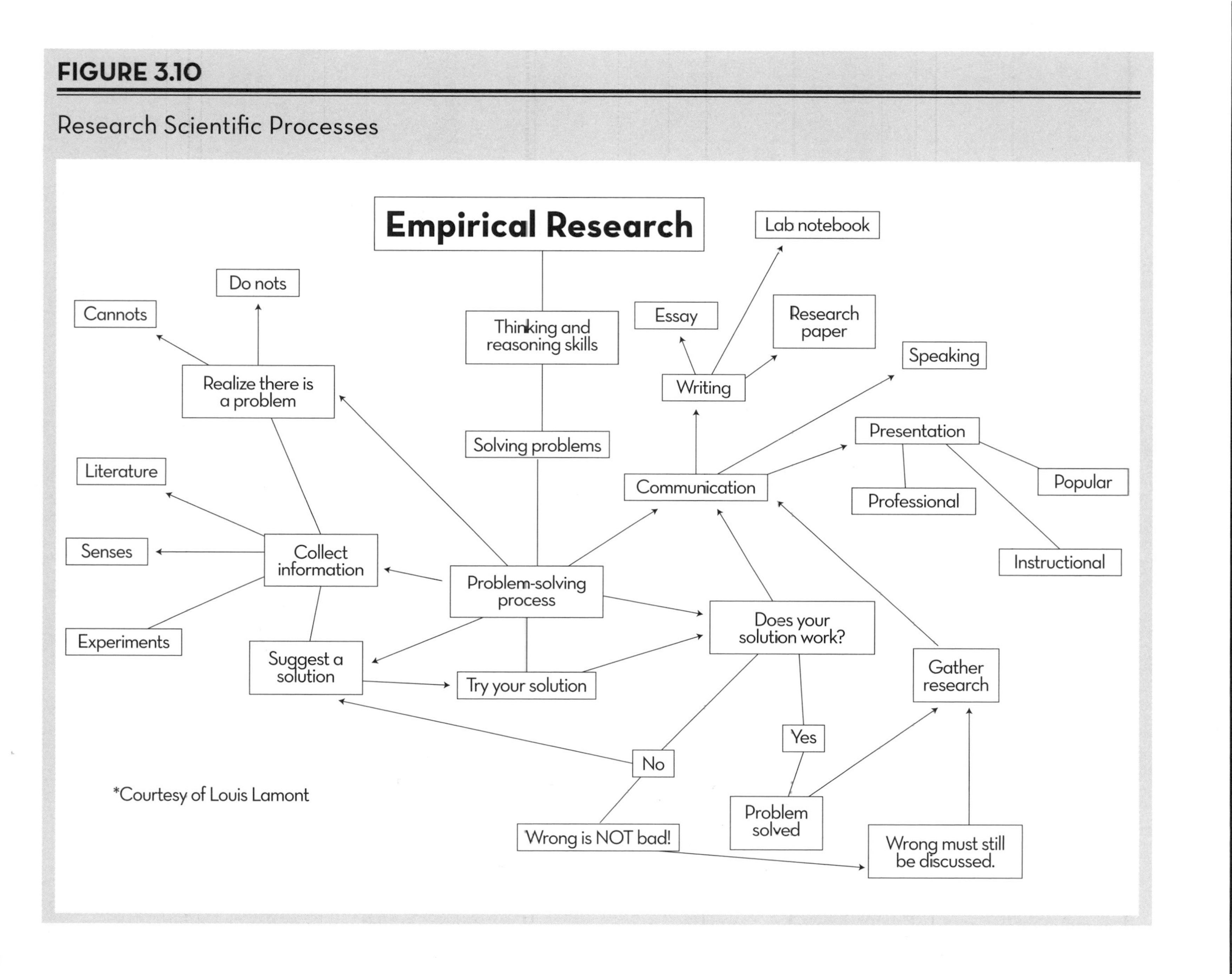

For this reason, teachers should refrain from using equation sheets and cheat sheets for all assessments. Students need to have the impetus to memorize the equations and concepts so memorization skills are in place. As was stated earlier, these skills are developed through practice and experience. In addition, students need to be forced to memorize processes as well as facts so they are ready to learn complex skills.

## References

AVID. 2006. AVID: Decades of college dreams. *www.avidonline.org.*

Blakemore, S., and U. Frith. 2005. *The learning brain: Lessons for education.* Malden, MA: Blackwell Publishing.

Bloom, B. S., ed. 1956. *Taxonomy of educational objectives, the classification of educational goals—Handbook I: Cognitive domain.* New York: McKay.

Boddy, N., K. Watson, and P. Aubusson. 2003. A trial of the five Es: A referent model for constructivist teaching and learning. *Research in Science Education* 33 (1): 27–42.

Bower, B., J. Lobdell, and L. Swenson. 1999. *History alive!: Engaging all learners in the diverse classroom.* 2nd rev. ed. Rancho Cordova, CA: Teachers Curriculum Institute.

bubbl.us. 2011. bubbl.us. *http://bubbl.us.*

Buell, J. 2009. *Closing the book on homework.* Philadelphia, PA: Temple University Press.

Bybee, R. W., et al. 2006. The BSCS 5E Instructional Model: Origins, effectiveness, and applications. BSCS. *www.bscs.org/pdf/bscs5eexecsummary.pdf.*

Center for Public Education. 2007. What research says about the value of homework: Research review. February 5. *www.centerforpubliceducation.org.*

Chanlin, L. 1997. The effects of verbal elaboration and visual elaboration on student learning. *International Journal of Instructional Media* 24 (4): 333–339.

CSCOPE. 2007. The 5E model of instruction. *http://pdspalooza.pbworks.com/f/ALL.pdf.*

Educational Technology. *http://www2.ed.gov/pubs/edtechprograms.*

Expert Panel Reviews. 2001, 2000. Modeling instruction in high school physics. Office of Educational Research and Improvement. U.S. Department of Education, Washington, DC. *http://www2.ed.gov/offices/OERI/ORAD/KAD/expert_panel/newscience_progs.html.*

Forehand, M. 2005. Bloom's taxonomy: Original and revised. Emerging Perspectives on Learning, Teaching, and Technology, ed. M. Orey. *http://projects.coe.uga.edu/epltt.*

Gorder, P. F. 2009. Study: Learning science facts doesn't boost science reasoning. *www.PhysOrg.com.*

Hestenes, D. 1987. Toward a modeling theory of physics instruction. *Am. J. Phys.* 55 (5): 440–454.

Hestenes, D. 1992. Modeling games in the Newtonian world. *Am. J. Phys.* 60: 732–748.

Hestenes, D. 1997. Modeling methodology for physics teachers. In *The changing role of the physics department in modern universities*, ed. E. Redish and J. Rigden. American Institute of Physics, Part II, 935–957. *http://modeling.asu.edu/R&E/Research.html.*

Hestenes, D. 2006. Notes for a modeling theory of science, cognition and instruction. Paper presented at the GIREP Conference, Modeling in Physics and Physics Education. Amsterdam, The Netherlands.

Inspiration Software, Inc. 2011. *www.inspiration.com.*

Institute for Human and Machine Cognition (IHMC). 2011. Cmap. *http://cmap.ihmc.us/conceptmap.html.*

Jackson, J., L. Dukerich, and D. Hestenes. 2008. Modeling instruction: An effective model for science education. *Science Educator* 17 (1): 10–17.

Johnson, D. W., R. T. Johnson, and E. J. Holubec. 1994. *Cooperative learning in the classroom.* Alexandria, VA: ASCD.

Jones, S. C. 1995. *Memory aids for math.* Fayetteville, AR: Educational Memory Aids.

June, H., and H. Huay. 2003. *Effectiveness of case studies: A survey of learners' perspectives and learning styles.* Singapore: Singapore Polytechnic.

Kagan, S. 1994. *Cooperative learning.* San Clemente, CA: Kagan Publishing.

Keates, N. *Wall Street Journal.* 2007. Schools turn down the heat on homework. January 19.

Kingore, B. 2004. *Differentiation: Simplified, realistic, and effective.* Austin, TX: Professional Associates Publishing.

Krathwohl, D. R. 2002. Revising Bloom's taxonomy. *Theory Into Practice* 41 (4): 212–218.

Make Sense Strategies. 2011. Masterminds Publishing LLC. *www.graphicorganizers.com.*

Math Mnemonics. 2011. Online Math Learning. *www.onlinemathlearning.com/math-mnemonics.html.*

Megowan-Romanowicz, C. 2010a. *Modeling instruction: How to do it!* Chinese Association of Physics Education Research. Beijing, China: Peoples Education Press.

Megowan-Romanowicz, C. 2010b. Modeling discourse in secondary science and mathematics classrooms. In *Modeling students' mathematical modeling competencies,* ed. R. A. Lesh, P. Galbraith, C. Haines, and A. Hurford, pp. 341–352. New York: Springer.

Megowan-Romanowicz, C. 2011. Helping students construct robust conceptual models. In *Models and modeling: Cognitive tools for scientific enquiry,* ed. M. S. Khine and I. M. Saleh, pp. 99–120. Dordrecht: Springer.

Mind Tools Ltd. 1996–2011. Mind Tools, Essential Skills for an Excellent Career. *www.mindtools.com.*

Mindmeister. 2011. Meisterlabs. *www.mindmeister.com.*

Mnemonic Devices. 2011. *www.ict4us.com/mnemonics.*

Muskingum. Learning Strategies Database. 2011. *www.muskingum.edu/~cal/database/general/notetaking.html.*

Nooriafshar, M., and T. N. Maraseni. 2005. A comparison of learning preferences and perceptions of high school students for statistics. Proceedings of the Hawaii International Conference on Statistics, Mathematics and Related Fields, pp. 760–768.

Pauk, W. 2001. *How to study in college.* 7th ed. Boston, MA: Houghton Mifflin.

Penn State. 2005. Too much homework can be counterproductive. *www.physorg.com.*

Penn State. 2007. Benefits of more homework vary across nations, grades. *ScienceDaily,* March 2. *www.sciencedaily.com /releases/2007/02/070227171018.htm.*

Sharp, C., W. Keys, and P. Benefield. 2001. Homework: A review of recent research. Slough: NFER. *http://education.qld.gov.au/review/pdfs/homework-text-for-web.pdf.*

Slavin, R. E. 1992. When and why does cooperative learning increase achievement? Theoretical and empirical perspectives. In *Interaction in cooperative groups: The theoretical anatomy of group learning,* ed. R. Hertz-Lazarowitz and N. Miller, pp. 145–173. New York: Cambridge University Press.

Susman, E. B. 1998. Cooperative learning: A review of factors that increase the effectiveness of cooperative computer-based instruction. *J. Educ. Comp. Res.* 18 (4): 303–322.

Thinking Maps, Inc. 2011. Thinking Maps. *www.thinkingmaps.com.*

Underwood, N. 2006. The teenage brain: Why adolescents sleep in, take risks, and won't listen to reason. *The Walrus,* November 2006. *www.walrusmagazine.com/articles/2006.11-science-the-teenage-brain.*

Wells, M., D. Hestenes, and G. Swackhamer. 1995. A modeling method for high school physics instruction. *Am. J. Phys.* 63: 606–619.

Ziegler, S. 1981. The effectiveness of cooperative learning teams for increasing cross-ethnic friendship: Additional evidence. *Human Orgaization* 40 (3): 264–268.

# CHAPTER 4

# From Concepts to Principles to Processes to Equations

## THE WAGON WASN'T INVENTED BEFORE THE WHEEL: LEARNING IN THE CORRECT ORDER

There is a tendency for students to misunderstand order and priorities when learning advanced mathematics and physical science. Many times students become so focused on the equations that they fail to comprehend the concepts and principles that underlie them.

The correct order for learning in mathematics and physical science is to start with the underlying concepts (definitions of variables) and progress to the principles (laws and relationships usually defined through laboratory explorations) to processes (step-by-step approaches to applying the principles) to equations (tools used within the application process).

Failure to learn these aspects in the correct order usually results in deficiencies and naive conceptions in a student's understanding of the material. Teachers must make sure their planned lessons follow this correct order so these deficiencies can be avoided.

## PRINCIPLES FROM CONCEPTS

When teaching a subject unit, concepts need to be learned and comprehended first. Many naive conceptions are connected to an insufficient understanding of the definitions of concepts. This insufficient understanding then propagates to the understanding of principles, processes, and equations of the unit.

As an example, students often develop confusion when learning the concepts of velocity and acceleration. Students often believe that an acceleration of zero means an object has zero velocity, a common error. This error can be traced to the similarity in form of the two definitions and insufficient exploration of the concepts and the relationship between them.

In science, only laboratory exploration of the concepts and relationships, coupled with sufficiently broad problem-solving practice, can build a true understanding of the concepts and avoid the typical naive conceptions.

## Processes Before Equations

Most students are obsessed with the equations, mistakenly believing they are the key to understanding concepts and relationships. In many ways, the contrary is true. The equations can actually hide the subtleties of the concepts and principles.

It is in the principle relationships and processes that true understanding lies. Teachers need to provide lesson plans that allow exploration of the relationships between concepts and enable students to comprehend and practice the processes by performing problem-solving practice.

Some reasons for the obsession with equations can be blamed on the presentation, both in classrooms and in textbooks. For students to understand the importance of relationships and processes, this pre-eminence must be stressed in the lessons. One suggestion is to stress relationship and processes before introducing equations, leaving the equations for the last steps of problem-solving mastery. Start with graphs and drawings and laboratory explorations, introducing only those equations that act as concept definitions (e.g., $\vec{v} = \Delta\vec{x}/\Delta t$ defines velocity).

What needs to be overcome is the tendency for students to look at problems as if they were formed from whole cloth. Teachers need to get students to see each problem as the application of processes (recipes) and tools (equations) for a given set of problems within a recognized conceptual unit (Newton's laws, for instance). This is the foundation of the problem-solving process presented in this book.

## Understanding Equations the Correct Way

When it is the proper time to consider equations, it is important that students are able to memorize equations and understand them at the fundamental and application levels. One technique that works well for maximizing the understanding of equations and math rules is to teach the student to memorize an equation or rule not in terms of symbols, but in words. For example, if a teacher asks a student to state Newton's second law of motion, he should not accept $F = ma$. The teacher should prompt the student to state the law in words with adequate detail: "The resultant force on an object is equal to the mass of the object multiplied by the acceleration of the object." Note that "Force equals mass times acceleration" is not acceptable, as it lacks appropriate detail to be fully descriptive of its applicability. Only after the student can correctly express the equation with words should the teacher have the student associate the expression with the equation in symbol form.

Another tool to enhance understanding of an equation and ease its correct application is the equation map. An equation map is a concept map that associates the symbols of an equation with their precise meanings. Each variable and symbol in an equation is linked to a bubble that gives the precise description of the variable in words, examples to elucidate the variables, alternate symbols, Standard International (SI) units, and domain and range

**FIGURE 4.1**

Example of an Equation Map

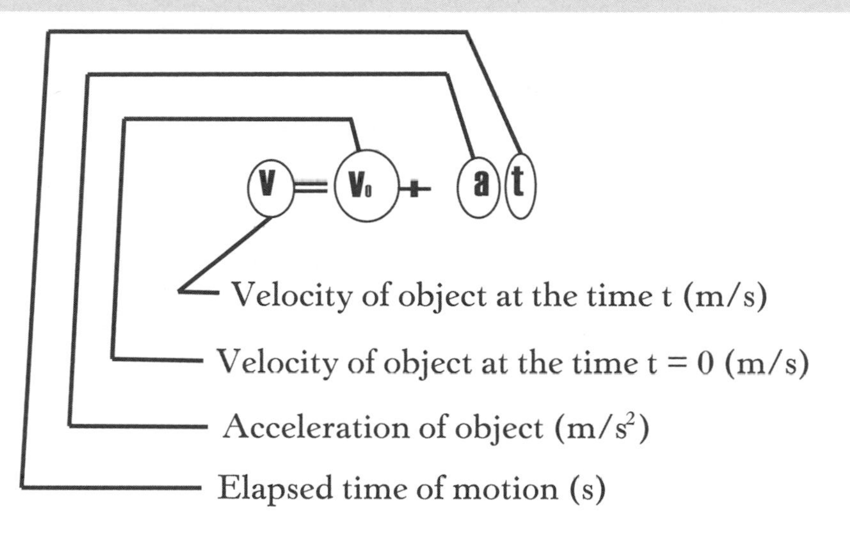


Applications:

1. Find the velocity of the object at time t given the initial velocity of the object, the acceleration of the object, and the elapsed time of the motion:
$$v = v_0 + a\ t$$
2. Find the initial velocity of the object given the velocity of the object at time t, the acceleration of the object, and the elapsed time of the motion:
$$v_0 = v - a\ t$$
3. Find the acceleration of the object given the initial velocity of the object, the velocity of the object at time t, and the elapse time of the motion:
$$a = (v - v_0) / t$$
4. Find the elapsed time of the motion given the initial velocity of the object, the velocity of the object at time t, and the acceleration of the object:
$$t = (v - v_0) / a$$

limits (if applicable; see Figure 4.1, p. 75). In addition, the map contains a detailed list of all the tasks that may be accomplished by using the equation with the specific algebraic form derived from the master equation. Finally, any limitations of the applicability of the equation should be stated (if applicable). Students should be encouraged to use these maps during problem-solving practice, as doing so will hone students' skills in associating the variables of their particular problem with the master variables of the equation. Then the proper replacements can be made to get the correct equations for the given problem. A rubric for grading equation maps is given in Appendix C.

If an adequate job has been done in learning and memorizing the definitions of the concepts within the equation (resultant force, mass, acceleration), then this effort will lead to a deeper understanding of the equation and its applicability in the problem-solving process.

## Multistage Assessment

Because we are advocating a staged approach to learning (concepts to principles to processes to equations), it only makes sense that this is mirrored in the assessment approach.

It is recommended that summative assessments be broken into two stages. The first stage should assess the student's knowledge and understanding of concepts and definitions of a unit. This would be followed by a reteaching strategy if necessary. The second-stage assessment should test understanding of principles and application of the principles to problem solving.

The benefit of this approach will be clear to anyone who has taught physics or physical science. Often, a student's inability to solve problems lies in their misunderstanding of the concepts involved. How can a student be expected to use equations if he doesn't understand the meaning of the variables? This staged assessment strategy ensures that concepts and definitions are understood adequately before the relationships between them are given and applied.

For example, let's say we are teaching kinematics. Concepts and definitions such as displacement, distance, average velocity, instantaneous velocity, speed, average acceleration, instantaneous acceleration, and elapsed time would be taught through various student-centered activities and then tested in the first-stage assessment. If reteaching is necessary, it can be done after the assessment. Then the principles (the four kinematic equations) and application problems may be introduced, learned, and practiced, leading to the second-stage assessment.

In this way, the progression from concept to principle to process to equation is mirrored in all aspects of the learning process, and the hierarchy becomes part of the student's understanding of the subject matter.

# CHAPTER 5

# Doing Calculations the Right Way

## Did You Ever Watch a Student Solve a Word Problem?

Observing a student trying to solve a word problem can often be a frustrating experience for the teacher. It is not uncommon for students to sit and stare at problems they do not understand, wasting valuable time in an unproductive trance. The first step in mitigating this behavior is to understand why students do this. When asked, many students will respond that they don't know where to start. The fact is that this behavior occurs because students don't perceive the processes necessary to successfully advance toward a solution.

### *Drooling and Panic*

The second stage after the trance occurs is when students begin to panic. This is an especially common occurrence during classroom assessments. Teachers observing this stage often see wandering eyes, tapping pencils, and panicked expressions as the clock advances. Progress is further impeded as the student's ability to concentrate is lost in the panic.

## Every Problem Is Treated Like It Is Unique.

There is a tendency for students to treat each problem as unique and requiring a unique approach to solve. This is rarely the truth of the matter in high school science and mathematics problem solving. The development of new processes and tools for problems is the regime of the professional scientist, not the high school student. Even the professionals know their goal isn't to solve a single problem, but to develop principles, tools, and processes that will allow them to better understand nature and attack new classes of problems. This same focus on principles and process, problem class over single problem, needs to drive the teaching of science and mathematics at all levels, including high school. Even though the tools and principles are already in place for the high school student, teachers should treat lessons as if the students are discovering them for the first time. The student should then be prompted to apply these tools and principles for a class of problems.

## Getting Students to See the Big Picture

The secret to getting students to learn processes is to set their perspective. They need to look at problems differently than their initial viewpoints: as a puzzle, not a problem; as a challenge, not a roadblock; and as a project, not a problem.

From this new perspective, the student is ready to learn a new approach to solving problems.

### *Motivating the Approach*

Here are four of the central motivators for developing a fully systematic problem-solving approach:

- To give a student a way of starting a problem even when the entire route to the solution isn't initially clear to the student
- To provide a partial view of the solution route to improve the student's confidence
- To allow for bookkeeping and check processes to eliminate mathematical manipulation and numerical mistakes
- To elicit higher-order thinking skills by honing systematic abilities and the ability to subdivide complex problems

Observations of students solving problems have demonstrated that if a student has the essential conceptual and specific procedural knowledge mastered, the student can successfully solve any problem if he or she can find a way to start it. Unfortunately, the tendency is for students to stare at problems when they don't see the entire path to the solution immediately. The trick is to get the student to think like Indiana Jones, discovering the solution during the general process (an adventure) instead of working a path already fully planned in their minds (a blueprint).

The procedure presented in this chapter gives the student a complete and general procedural approach for executing any calculation from the beginning to the end: The Method. This general procedure can be integrated with subprocedures that are specific to different types of problems to form a repeatable process for solution of problems of a given class. With practice, The Method has been found to be an effective tool for improving a student's problem-solving prowess and increasing the student's confidence during the process.

### *Problem Solving Is Like Using Tools to Build a House or Bake a Cake.*

Teachers need to prompt their students to look at equations as tools or utensils. A screwdriver is a tool, but it cannot build a cabinet alone. Without a plan and other tools, the cabinet will never be constructed. Even worse, we need to know what a screwdriver is used for, when to use it, and when it isn't the appropriate tool. We never want to observe the cabinetmaker using a screwdriver to hammer nails.

As science and mathematics teachers, we see this kind of misuse of equations by students on a regular basis. If you watch these students work, the equation or equations are often the first thing they write down. In doing so, they pick their tools before they have set their goals or plans. This would be inappropriate in carpentry and cooking, and it is inappropriate in problem solving.

### *Monkey See, Monkey Do!*

If the teacher wants to teach his students to see and follow processes, it is important that the teacher model how to use the processes during the teaching of problem solving. This should entail following the process religiously and describing the solution in terms of the process as the teacher works, avoiding any tendency to cut corners. Modeling two or three problems of a given type gives the students a template to follow in their own solutions of similar problems.

It is a good idea to allow the student access to the process and subprocess descriptions in written form during the early stages of mastering the techniques. These written plans provide a prompt to force students to follow the process. Later, this crutch can be removed as the student attains mastery of the processes.

## How to Calculate: The Method

In this section, the steps of The Method will be presented in detail. They may seem to be a bit complex at first but will become clarified as examples are presented later. For teachers to successfully use The Method in their teaching, they must become familiar with the steps and practice them beforehand for various problem types that they will teach. For some simple problems, the steps may seem like overkill, especially for the experienced teacher. Still, teachers must keep in mind that the goal is to provide the students with a tool that will result in good problem-solving habits when they approach more complex problems. Teachers will want their students to follow the steps and become comfortable with them, so the teacher needs to be able to model the steps for the student for a variety of cases.

### Setting the Foundation

Before we begin to outline the steps, it is essential for the teacher to understand that The Method is not a system to teach concepts and principles. It is strictly a process for effective problem solving. The foundational knowledge, in the form of concepts, principles, laws, and equations, must be in place beforehand. The teacher should spend the time to make sure the student has a firm grasp on these concepts, principles, laws, and equations before attempting application to a problem. In addition, any specific subprocesses that are unique to a given learning unit must be explained to the students. These processes are integrated into the general process of The Method.

This foundation setting may be accomplished through a combination of laboratory explorations, demonstrations, and virtual simulations with an emphasis on guided self-exploration and discussion of subtleties and potential naïve conceptions. The use of graphic organizers, as explained in Chapter 2, can be of great benefit in setting this foundation and integrating it into memory.

### Not Equations—Process!

It is useful for the teacher to explain to the students beforehand that he or she will attempt to de-emphasize the importance of equations and emphasize the importance of processes. The teacher must make the students understand that they should not start a problem by writing equations and that doing so will result in loss of grade. This may seem harsh, but the teacher must keep in mind that he or she may be trying to undo years of incorrect problem-solving habits that are ingrained in the students' thought processes, an often challenging task in itself.

## The Steps of The Method

We present the steps of The Method below. The motivation for its development was the formulation of a fully systematic approach to solving mathematical word problems that requires minimal guesswork, does not require the student to see the whole of the solution before starting, and has checks built in to the process.

Teachers will note that some of the steps are much like those presented in many textbooks. However, steps have been added and others modified so that the process contains bookkeeping techniques for easing algebraic manipulation and checks for avoiding algebraic and numerical errors.

### Step 1: Read It!

**Read the problem twice. Underline or highlight important information such as numerical data, units, assumptions, and what information is requested.**

Two of the biggest obstacles that students must overcome to successfully solve these problems are the correct interpretation of what they are reading and the efficient extraction of all useful information in the problem statement.

The first reading of the problem, the passive one, is designed to give the student a general idea of what is being requested. The second active reading of the problem is designed to allow the efficient and complete extraction of useful information. By using a pen or highlighter to delineate important data, facts, and assumptions, students are less likely to miss important information necessary to solve the problem or misinterpret what information is sought.

One good approach is to read each sentence individually and extract the information one sentence at a time. In this way, nothing is missed. Note that some sentences may have no pertinent information for the solution, while others may contain assumptions but no numerical data.

Furthermore, the student should look for key words and phrases that imply operations that will be performed. For example, "increased by" implies addition, "out of" implies division, and "yields" implies equality. These phrases can be noted by the student to use later in the solution process.

In the early stages of learning The Method, the teacher can assist the students as they learn to extract the relevant data from a problem's text by writing the extracted information, numerical data, and assumptions on the board as the students delineate it.

## *Step 2: Plan It!*

**Map or list important concepts, definitions, laws, and principles you will need for the problem.**

Once a student has delineated the important information from the word problem, they must then connect that information to concepts, definitions, laws, and principles they will use in the problem solving. It is useful at this point in the process to have the students list or map concepts, definitions, laws, and principles they believe will get them to the solution, with justification statements for their choices.

Students should become familiar with key words or problems and their commonly associated principles. As an example, if the problem statement discusses forces and acceleration (constant), the student might conclude that they can apply Newton's second law of motion as it contains the concepts of the problem. Another example for mathematics is given by the map in Figure 5.1 (p. 82).

As yet another physics example, a student might conclude that a problem containing a roller coaster with friction should use the generalized work-energy principle. See Appendix D for a list of key terms and problems by physics topic and Appendix E for a list of key terms and meaning for mathematics.

Sometimes, on particularly complex problems, the student may need to list several principles they will apply in the solution. This step focuses the student's mind on the tools they need for later steps in the solution process.

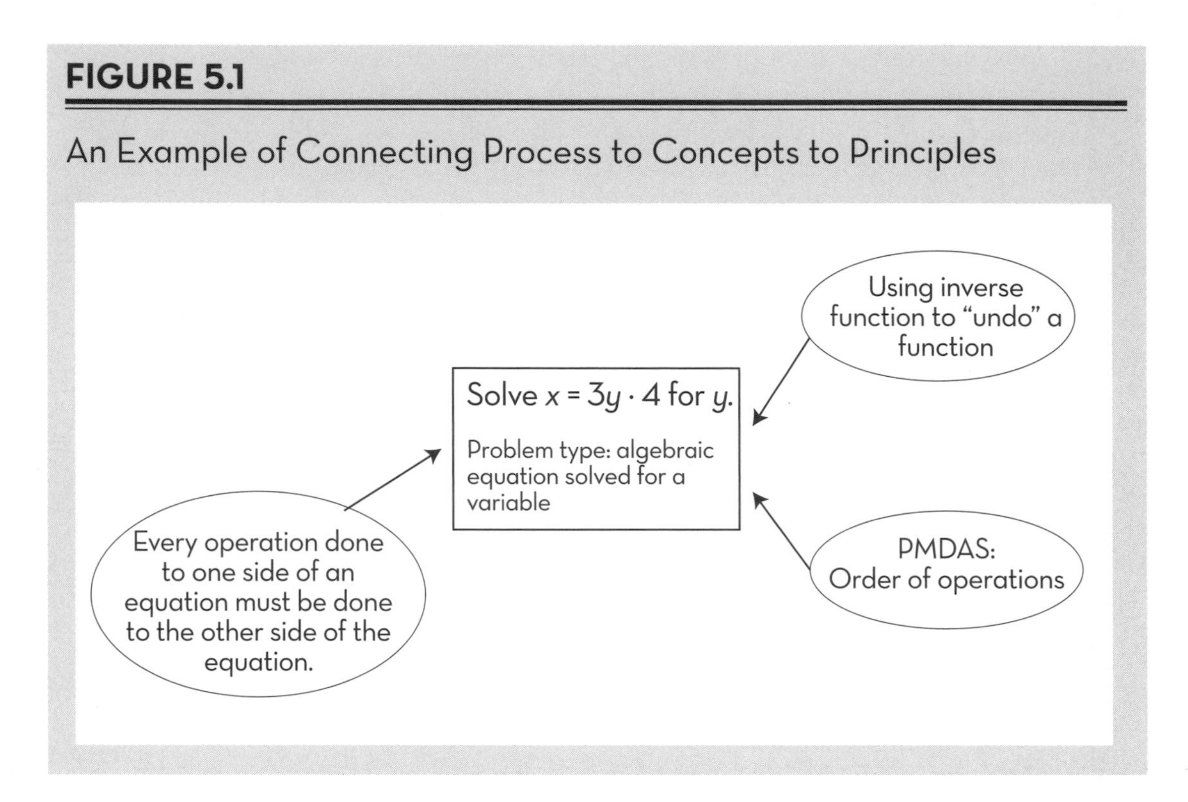


FIGURE 5.1

An Example of Connecting Process to Concepts to Principles

Students should be encouraged to consider previously solved problems from the same unit in this step so commonalities may be found and comprehended. In this way, students begin to understand that problems in the same unit use the same specific processes and tools for solution, thus building real comprehension of the concepts and principles involved.

As students become more confident with their knowledge and skills in a unit, this step may be pared back or eliminated. In addition, this step can be performed once for a set of problems involving the same principles to avoid unnecessary repetition. It should be noted that this step can be especially important when preparing for a test involving many learning units (like an AP test) because these tests require the students to recognize the first principles they must use to solve the given problems. Indeed, some problems may contain principles from different learning units.

### *Step 3: Draw It!*

Construct a drawing (if appropriate). This is an important step in the solution of geometry-based problems (geometry, trigonometry, precalculus, calculus, physics). Drawings elucidate problem content.

1. Drawings should be large enough and neat enough to be useful during problem solving (quarter-page minimum for detailed drawings).

2. Drawings should be labeled with variables and values with units.
3. Some solutions may require more than one drawing or new drawings or alterations to the existing drawings to be constructed during the solution process.
4. Some problems, especially in physics, should have appropriately assigned and labeled coordinate axes and origins.

Not all problems are amenable to a drawing. But when a drawing will work, there is no better tool for organizing the information and a student's thinking process than a complete drawing. Drawings provide an intermediate step between the textual content of a word problem and the mathematical expressions of the solution. Students often find that if they can reduce the word problem to a drawing, their understanding of the problem and what is needed for solution is enhanced.

Notice the four attributes listed above. These attributes constitute what should be considered a minimally adequate drawing. The drawing, if complete, should replace the problem statement and can be an active part of the solution process. Once the drawing is finished, the student should not have to look back at the problem statement again, but may make alterations to the drawing during the solution process as needed. Attribute 4 is often skipped by students, but it is critical in any physics problem that involves vector quantities so that proper signs may be given in equations and numerical data.

The drawing is more than an illustration; it is a tool. The student should be encouraged to refer back to the drawing often during the rest of the process. It is common for some types of problems to have to modify a drawing or produce new drawings during the course of a solution.

Early in the process of learning The Method, the teacher should model the production of good drawings for the students. From these demonstration drawings, students will observe the parts that a good drawing should contain and produce better drawings as they work problems themselves.

Students often need a significant amount of practice producing good drawings. One technique that teachers can use is to give students problem statements and instruct them to produce a good drawing with all of the attributes without actually working the problem. Use of colored pencils (or tablet computer palette and stylus)—with each color used for a different aspect of the drawing (red for axes, blue for known variables, brown for unknown variables, etc.)—can help students become better at producing complete drawings. When the teacher demonstrates drawings on the board, they should use colored chalk or markers to encourage students to use this technique.

Teachers need to be stringent about grading drawings, as this is the step in the process where students are most likely to take a shortcut.

## Step 4: List What You Know!

List known data: Assign each number in a problem a meaningful variable name and write, <var name> = <number> <unit>. Make sure correct significant figures are carried (e.g., $V_1 = 27.2$ m/s).

The known data would include any numerical information in the problem statement plus any constants that might be required. Variable names need to be reasonable. This means they need to be descriptive of the data type and conform to conventions. For example, $v$ can represent a velocity or volume but should not be used to represent acceleration, as that would violate known conventions. In cases where there is more than one variable of the same type, subscripts can be used. For example, $v_i$ can represent an initial velocity and $v_f$ can represent a final velocity. There is substantial freedom in naming variables within the conventions; however, variable names should always be as descriptive as possible to avoid confusion later in the solution. For instance, if we are labeling the mass of a truck, $m_T$ is a better label than $m_1$ because we could forget what the 1 subscript represents during the numerical substitutions. Keep in mind that the variable names, if chosen within conventions and with care, can and should provide clues to the equations that will be needed for the solution.

Teachers need to stress the importance of putting units on the numbers at all steps in the solution, starting with this step, so that unit errors can be avoided. Note that this is a good step in the process to perform any unit conversions necessary for the solution.

If a drawing was used in the previous step, this list should be written into the drawing. If a given variable is associated with an object in the drawing, the student should be encouraged to place the data statement close to or on the object as a way to increase the usefulness of the drawing, by giving a visible association between object and variable.

If a drawing is not appropriate for the problem, then this data can be given in a column list with the word *knowns* at the top.

## Step 5: List What You Want to Find.

List unknown(s). Assign each of the quantities being solved for a meaningful variable name and write <var name> = ? <unit> (e.g., $P_1$ = ? atm).

This step is similar to the previous one, except that the values are replaced with a "?" It may seem trivial, but this step provides a visual cue to the student regarding the goal of the solution. In particularly complex problems, students can often lose track of their target purpose and go off on tangents. It is the purpose of this step to provide a reminder of this goal or goals later in the process.

As with the knowns, variable names should be reasonable and follow established conventions. Also as with the knowns, the importance of including the unit should be stressed. It is not uncommon for a problem to require an answer with a particular type of unit. The student may require a visual reminder of this. For example, the calculation of a pressure may give the answer in kilopascals, but the question asks for the answer in atmospheres. The unit atm in the unknown statement reminds the student to perform the unit conversion. If the student suspects that he will need to do a unit conversion of the unknown at the end of the solution, writing down a reminder in the form of the conversion factor can be done on or near the unknown statement.

As with the knowns, the unknowns can be included in the drawing, if a drawing is used for the problem. As before, students should associate an unknown statement with the correct object in the drawing, if appropriate. If a drawing is not used, the statement(s) should be in a column list under the heading *unknowns*.

### Step 6: List the Right Equations in the Right Order.

Using the concepts, laws, and principles of step 2 as guidance, list appropriate equations for the solution:

A. First, write equation(s) containing the "unknown(s)" in terms of variables in your "known" list and using your chosen variable names.
B. Algebraically solve the equation(s) for the "unknown(s)" (if necessary). Never substitute numbers before manipulating equation(s). This causes transcription errors.
C. Analyze each equation after expression: Place a question mark over each variable that is an unknown and a check mark over each variable that is on the list of knowns.
D. Two cases can occur at this point (possibly both together):
    a. If a variable has neither mark over it, a new equation must be given that contains this new "intermediate unknown" variable. This should occur for each intermediate unknown in an equation.
    b. If the equation contains $n$ of the unknowns with a question mark on them ($n \geq 2$), $n$-1 additional equations must be written that contain one or more of these unknowns.
E. Repeat substeps A through D recursively for these new equations, assuming the "intermediate unknown" is the new "unknown." Stop when no new "intermediate unknowns" occur and there is an equation for each of the original unknowns.

If appropriate, equations may be combined algebraically before numeric substitution to simplify evaluation. Sometimes this must be done—such as when only variable combinations (ratios, for instance) are known but not the values of the individual variables, or when expressions, not numbers, are the goal of the problem.

This is where the solution process defined here diverges most sharply from the process presented in most books. In standard presentations of solution processes, the equations are simply listed with no regard to the order of evaluation, and no hint of whether the set is complete. Following the five steps listed above yields a complete list of necessary equations, in the correct order of evaluation, and in the correct form for solution. Note that the process is a recursive cycle, ending only when all the necessary equations are found.

Students should be encouraged to use the equation maps presented earlier (see Figure 4.1, p. 75) to match their chosen variable names with the correct variables in the master equations. This can help alleviate one of the more difficult tasks in problem solving, which is writing the correct equation in terms of the particular variables in the problem. If the student has done a good job of picking variable names and has associated the variables spatially with objects within the drawing, the correspondence with the master variables in the mapped equation should be easily identified.

It should also be noted that some equations can simply be listed right from the concepts and principles, while others might need to be derived from the concepts, principles, and information contained in or extracted from the drawing. Again, the drawing is important, as it acts as an active tool in the solution of this type of problem.

### *Step 7: Solve It!*

Substitute values of "knowns" into equations with units. Perform this process on paper before using the calculator:

- Start with the last equation(s) written and work to the first. Substitute each evaluated "intermediate unknown" into the next equation above. Note: Solve any systems of equations that occur in the list using elimination or substitution methods.
- The units are important! Perform dimensional analysis on each equation after substitution. Any further unit conversions necessary may be performed at this step. Check to make sure the intermediate and final unknowns have the correct units. This is a great ongoing check that you are doing the problem correctly. Algebra and equation mistakes can be found early.
- Evaluate with a calculator only after doing a dimensional analysis check on paper. Use rules for significant digit manipulation.

Students tend to want to cut this step short by going straight to the calculator. Teachers need to be aware of this practice and discourage it. Most calculators lack the ability to check units. This check provides an excellent method for circumventing mistakes in writing down equations, performing algebra, and avoiding incorrect substitutions. In addition, students will often do this step on paper, but place units only on the answer. This also loses the benefit of the units check. Units should be placed on every substituted number so that dimensional analysis can be performed.

Finally, it is important that science teachers stress the importance and proper manipulation of significant digits. Given that laboratory results are the basis of all scientific claims, we should never separate the idea of precision from our calculations. Failure to do so can result in improper precision evaluation in laboratory work.

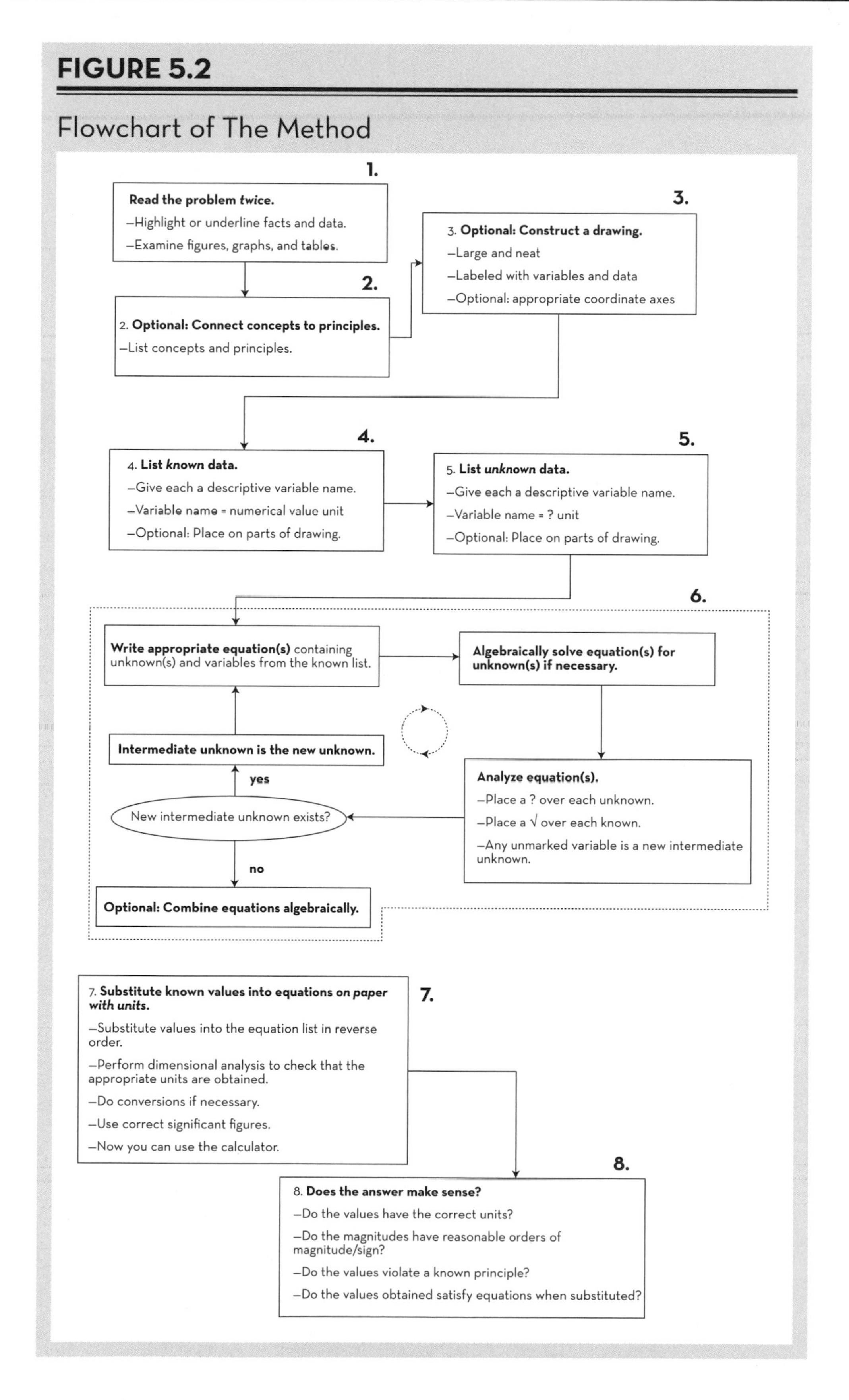


**FIGURE 5.2**

Flowchart of The Method

### Step 8: Check It!

Check to see if the "unknown" value(s) obtained make sense:

- Do the values obtained have the correct units?
- Do the magnitude(s) of the value(s) obtained conform to reasonable orders of magnitude and sign?
- Do the values violate a known principle?
- Do the values give good results when substituted back into the equations?

As a student's understanding of the subject increases in sophistication with time, he or she will be able to check the reasonableness of the answer by a variety of additional checks, including higher-order considerations such as symmetry and perturbative methods.

A flowchart of the entire process of The Method is given in Figure 5.2 (p. 87), showing the eight steps and their implementation. Students should be encouraged to have the flowchart available during problem solution as a guide, especially when The Method is first introduced.

## OK, So You Have Taught The Method ...

So now that the teacher has taught The Method, the student will become an expert problem solver, right? Not necessarily. Teaching The Method requires an effective approach and a commitment to follow-up. The instructional approach should include the following considerations.

### Yet Again, Monkey See, Monkey Do!

A teacher cannot expect students to buy into The Method if the teacher does not buy into it. Teachers must use The Method in example problems that they present to the class to demonstrate the process and convince the students of The Method's effectiveness.

The goal is to have the student follow the steps without cutting corners, so it is important for the teacher to avoid cutting corners when presenting problem solutions. For students to become truly proficient and benefit from the advantages of the process, they need to be convinced to do all the steps. Since The Method can result in a bit more writing than usual, teachers must be adamant about the importance of completeness during solution presentation. This is best reinforced by setting a good example.

What eventually becomes clear to students is that as they become proficient in the process, they actually save time and improve their grades by following The Method. These benefits come from avoiding mistakes and wasted time during the process, despite the extra writing. But to get to this conclusion, the student must be led by the teacher through consistent practice.

### *Patience, Patience, Patience*

It takes time and practice for students to become comfortable with the steps. Teachers need to be patient during this period of adjustment. It is easy for a teacher to become frustrated with the pace of this process. Some students will build mastery and comfort faster than others. Teachers can ease this process through a program of encouragement and incentives, but what teachers should not do is circumvent the process prematurely, as this will have adverse effects on the problem-solving skills by sowing seeds of confusion in students' minds.

One good idea is to let students work on problems in cooperative groups, where the group is composed of students of varying ability. Students solve problems with the goal of making sure that every member of the group understands the solution. This has been found to be effective in accelerating the pace at which the student masters The Method as students bring their own strengths to the process. This can be especially beneficial to students who have deficiencies in the language arts as it provides dynamic assistance that can aid in circumventing these difficulties.

### *Consistency Is Key.*

Consistency is the key to success. Teachers must insist on consistent application of The Method for students to build mastery and confidence with it. If students are introduced to the steps of The Method in early problem-solving courses, the mastery of it can build naturally as the complexity and sophistication of problems presented to students increase. In this way, the problem-solving skills are in place before the more challenging problems are given.

### *No Shortcuts*

Teachers should be aware that students have a tendency to skip steps in the process. Teenage nature being what it is, students will often attempt to get away with as little work as possible. Because The Method requires a bit of extra writing, students will try to take shortcuts to avoid the extra work. It is essential that teachers keep on top of this tendency and discourage it, and it is recommended that teachers grade, at least in part, on completeness to build good habits.

## Examples of The Method in Action

The steps of The Method can seem a bit complicated and intimidating in written form. In practice, they aren't nearly that difficult. With patience and consistency of usage, the students will develop a level of comfort and confidence and get faster incrementally. They will also realize that the number of mistakes decreases compared to their performance before using the technique.

## A Geometry/Algebra Example: Calculating the Dimensions of a Rectangle From the Area and Perimeter

Let's start with an algebraic geometry problem that will involve a simple drawing in the solution. The problem is stated as follows:

The area of a rectangle is 20 $m^2$ and the perimeter is 18 m. What are the length and width of this rectangle?

- Step 1: Read the problem passively and then actively.

The area of a rectangle is 20 $m^2$ and the perimeter is 18 m. What are the length and width of this rectangle?

The underlined material will be used to define the variables and their values.

- Step 2: Here is a list of concepts that may be part of this problem's solution:
    - Rectangle
    - Area
    - Perimeter
    - Volume

Here is a list of the principles, definitions, and laws that will be involved:

- Equation for area of a rectangle
- Equation for perimeter of a rectangle

This list will be the basis of the formation of the equations in Step 6. Again, as students become more comfortable with the process, this step may be dropped.

- Step 3: The graphic for this problem isn't complicated (see Figure 5.3). The variable names meet standard conventions and are associated with the appropriate parts of the drawing by their close proximity. Note also that units are given for all variables and a question mark in place of a value designates the two unknowns of the problem, $L$ and $W$.
- Steps 4 and 5: Because we have constructed a drawing for this problem and the variables are placed on it, these two steps are already complete.
- Step 6: List two equations that contain the unknowns and come from our concept and principle list of step 2:

$$A = L \times W \qquad P = 2L + 2W$$

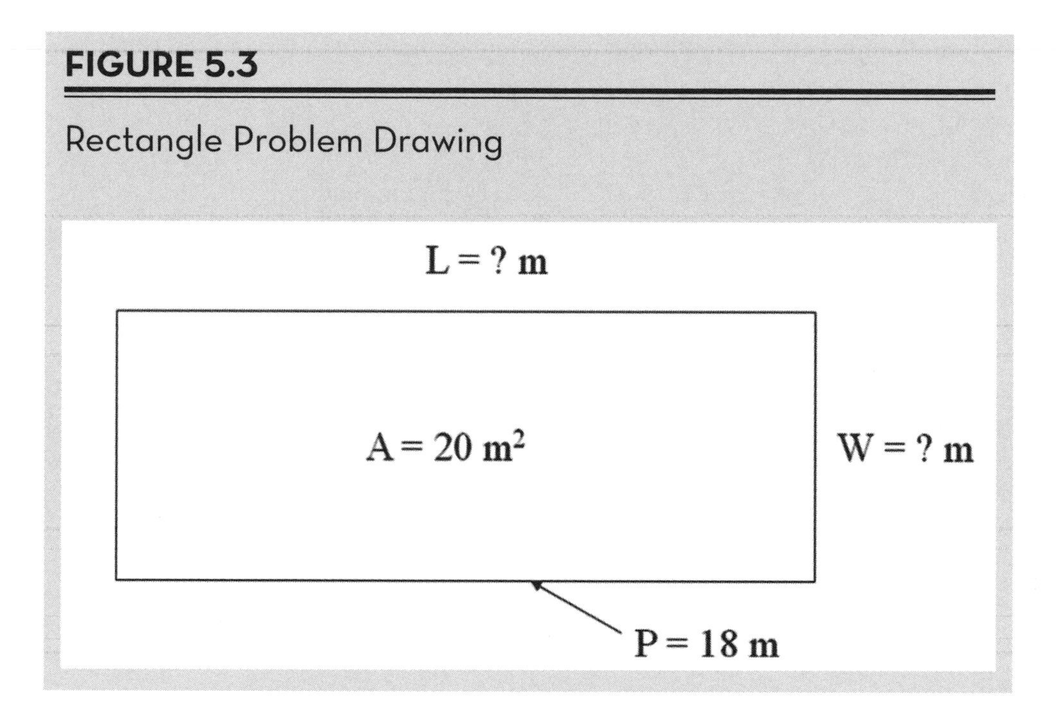


**FIGURE 5.3**

Rectangle Problem Drawing

These two equations, the equations for area and perimeter of a rectangle, form a system of equations for $L$ and $W$ and come directly from the list of concepts and principles in step 2. Now the equations are analyzed, placing a "?" on the unknown and a "√" on each known listed on the drawing:

$$(1)\ \overset{\surd}{A} = L \times \overset{?}{W} \qquad\qquad (2)\ \overset{\surd}{P} = 2\overset{?}{L} + 2\overset{?}{W}$$

Note that neither of these equations has unmarked variables. When there are no new intermediate unknowns, we know we have enough equations for the solution. We now have the complete set of equations, (1) and (2), which, because they are a system of equations, must be combined algebraically for solution. We begin by solving equation (1) for $L$ to get equation (1'):

$$L = A/W \qquad (1')$$

Then we substitute this equation into equation (2) to reduce the problem to one equation for the single variable $W$:

$$P = 2\,(A/W) + 2W$$

Multiplying the whole equation by $W$ and rearranging terms, we get a quadratic equation for $W$:

$$2W^2 - PW + 2A = 0 \qquad (2')$$

Before we use the quadratic formula to complete the solution, it should be stressed that students often have problems seeing patterns in equations such as the one we have here, especially if they must be manipulated to match a standard form (the quadratic form $Ax^2 + Bx + C$, in this case). Not all students will be able to do this, and teachers must have patience as students' skills in this area mature.

Applying the quadratic formula to equation (2'), we find the solution for $W$ *given* by equation (2"):

$$W = [P \pm (P^2 - 16A)^{1/2}]/4 \qquad (2")$$

This equation (2"), along with equation (1') for $L$, are used for the numerical evaluation in step 7.

- Step 7: The equations of step 6 are now evaluated in reverse order, (2") and then (1'). First we evaluate equation (2"):

  $$W = (18\ m \pm ((18\ m)^2 - 16(20\ m^2))^{1/2})/4 \qquad (2")$$

  This yields the following solution:

  $W$ = 4m or 5m.

  Substituting each value into equation (1') yields:

  $L = (20m^2/4m)$ or $(20m^2/5m)$

  or

  $L$ = 5m or 4m.

Note that the numbers have been substituted into the equations with correct units and dimensional analysis has been performed to check that the equations are correct.

- Step 8: To check the answer, we have symmetry as our guide. We expect the length and width to be interchangeable by the symmetry of the area equation and perimeter equation. Therefore, the interchange of values for the two solutions, $L$ and $W$, makes sense. Also, the two value sets each satisfy the two equations when substituted back into them.

## *A Physics Example: An Inclined Plane Problem*

Let us consider a sample problem from physics. This problem was chosen because it demonstrates all of the steps in the process and demonstrates the need for alteration of the basic drawing during analysis. Note that the solution will seem overly long because the steps are being described as they are demonstrated. Don't worry—actual solutions are not nearly this long. Here is the problem:

A box with a mass of 500.0 kg is stationary on an inclined plane with an inclination angle of 22°. Find the coefficient of friction for the plane.

- Step 1: After the problem is read quickly, the problem must be reread actively, one sentence at a time. Here is an example of the problem read actively:

A box with a mass of 500.0 kg is stationary on an inclined plane with an inclination angle of 22°. Find the coefficient of friction for the plane.

The underlined material is used to define the variables and values when the drawing is constructed.

- Step 2: Now is the time to think about the concepts and principles involved in the problem. Here is a list of concepts that may be part of the problem:

**FIGURE 5.4**

Inclined Plane Problem Drawing

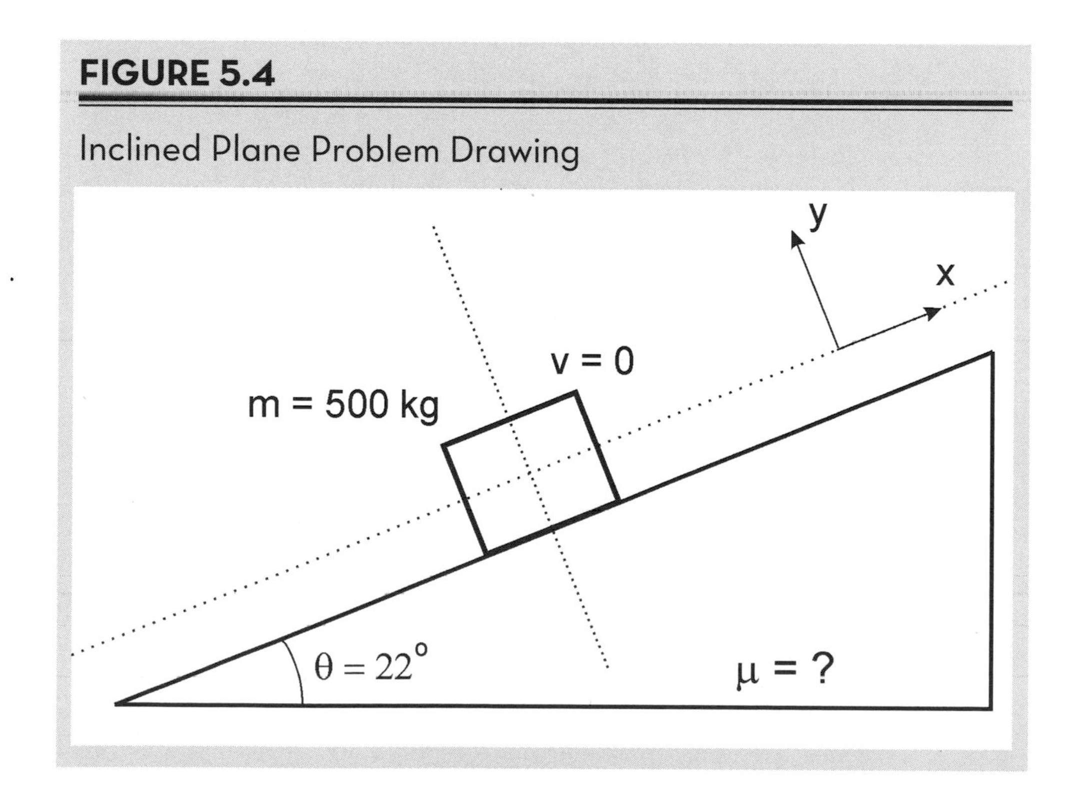

- Inclined plane
- Gravity force
- Normal force
- Coefficient of friction
- Free-body diagram

Here is a list of the principles, definitions, and laws that will be used:

- Newton's first law of motion in two dimensions
- Definition of weight
- Definition of friction force

This list will be the basis of the formation of the equations in step 6. As stated before, as students become more comfortable with the process, this step may be eliminated.

- Step 3: Let's formulate the basic drawing for this problem (see Figure 5.4, p. 93).

Note that the drawing includes all of the variables stated in the problem statement, knowns and unknowns, with sensible variable names, units, and numerical values for the knowns and a question mark in place of the value for the unknown. They are written into the drawing so they are in proximity of the related object or material. Furthermore, axes have been placed in the drawing to define the direction of positive vectors. Note that the axes are oriented relative to the incline. This allows for less geometric analysis later.

The student should be able to work the problem now without looking back at the problem statement. This is a key to the strength of The Method. Research has demonstrated that most students can understand a problem in graphical form more clearly than in verbal form.

This step allows for alterations to the drawing or for new drawings to be formulated. These drawings assist in the process of extracting the equations from the principles. To implement Newton's first law for this problem, a free-body diagram is formed. It can be placed on the original drawing or formed as a new drawing, as shown in Figure 5.5.

- Steps 4 and 5: These steps are skipped for this problem as we use a drawing. The knowns and unknowns are already integrated into the drawing.
- Step 6: The equations are listed, starting with an equation containing the unknown, the coefficient of friction μ, $F_f = \mu F_N$, where $F_f$ is the friction force on the box and $F_N$ is the normal force on the box. This equation is the definition of the friction force and is listed in step 2.
  Let us solve this equation for μ and place a question mark on the unknown μ:

$$\mu^{?} = F_f / F_N \qquad (1)$$

**FIGURE 5.5**

Inclined Plane Problem Free-Body Diagram

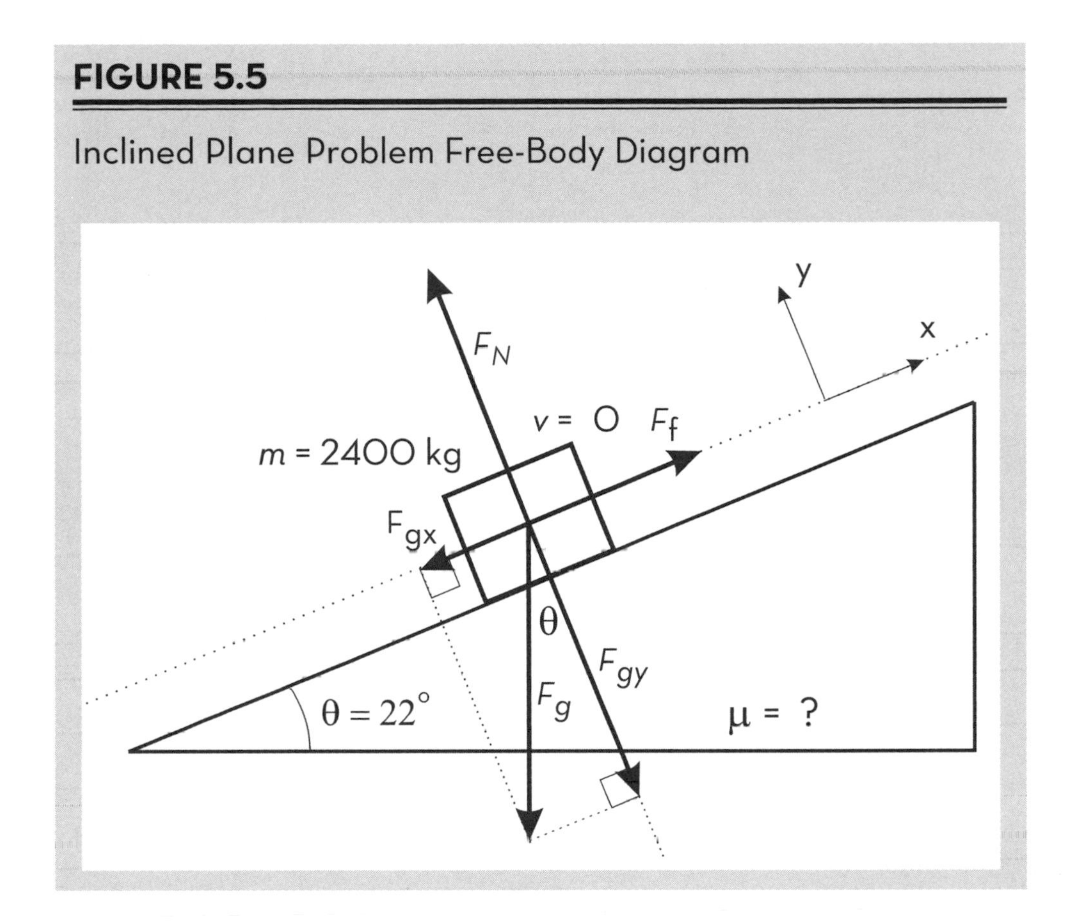


Notice that the two forces are unchecked. This means that they are both intermediate unknowns, and each requires a new equation.

To obtain these two equations, a free-body diagram must be constructed from the original drawing. Components of all the forces on the box that are not already along axes must be determined from the geometry of the diagram. In this case, the only force that requires the taking of components is the gravitational force $\vec{F}_g$ (see Figure 5.5). This allows us to split Newton's first law in 2 dimensions from step 2:

$$\sum \vec{F} = 0$$

into two component form equations in *x* and *y*:

$$\sum F_x = 0 \qquad \sum F_y = 0$$

Using the free-body diagram and the force components, these equations become:

$$F_f - F_{gx} = 0 \qquad F_N - F_{gy} = 0,$$

In the equations, $F_{gx}$ and $F_{gy}$ are the $x$ and $y$ components of the gravitational force, respectively.

Solving these equations for the intermediate unknowns gives us the two equations we need that we mark up with "?" and "√" as before:

$$\overset{?}{F_f} = F_{gx} \quad (2) \qquad \overset{?}{F_N} = F_{gy} \quad (3)$$

Note that $F_{gx}$ and $F_{gy}$ are not checked. This means that we need two more equations for these two intermediate unknowns. These equations come from the trigonometry of the component construction from the free-body diagram in Figure 5.5:

$$F_{gx} = F_g \sin \theta$$

and

$$F_{gy} = F_g \cos \theta$$

These two equations require no algebraic manipulation, as they are already solved for the intermediate unknowns. Marking these two equations gives us the next two equations of the solution set:

$$\overset{?}{F_{gx}} = \overset{?}{F_g} \, sin \, \overset{\surd}{\theta} \qquad (4)$$

and

$$\overset{?}{F_{gy}} = F_g \, cos \, \overset{\surd}{\theta} \qquad (5)$$

Finally, we note that $F_g$ is unchecked, which means that it is an intermediate unknown requiring another equation. This equation comes from the definition of the gravitational force:

$$F_g = mg$$

In this equation, $g$ is the acceleration due to gravity ($g$ = 9.8 m/s²). No algebraic manipulation is necessary. Marking this equation gives the final equation of the solution set:

$$\overset{?}{F_g} = \overset{\surd}{m}\overset{\surd}{g} \qquad (6)$$

- Step 7: The six equations of step 6 are now evaluated. In this case, it is simpler to combine all the equations, substituting equation (6) into equations (4) and (5), then substituting those into equations (2) and (3). These two resulting equations are then substituted into equation (1) to get the following:

$$\mu = \tan \theta$$

Substituting for the incline angle θ, we get

$$\mu = \tan 22°$$

or

$$\mu = 0.40$$

Note that there is no unit for this coefficient as expected.

- Step 8: Now, we check the answer. There are no units as expected. We expect the value of the coefficient of friction to be between 0 and 1. The equation makes sense, as it says that the coefficient grows as the incline angle increases.

### A Physics Example: Calculating Buoyancy

Let us consider an example problem from another branch of physics. This problem was chosen because it demonstrates all the steps in the process and requires multiple principles to be invoked. Note again that the solution will seem to be long because of the explanation text. Here is the problem:

A 250,000 kg iceberg floats in the ocean. What volume of the iceberg is above the water line? Assume a density for the saltwater ice of 0.920 kg/m$^3$ and a saltwater density of 1.024 kg/m$^3$.

- Step 1: The first step instructs the problem solver to read the problem over twice, the first time quickly and the second time actively. The second time the problem is read, the reader highlights or underlines important information to extract, one sentence at a time. Here is the text of the problem read actively:

A <u>250,000 kg iceberg</u> floats in the ocean. <u>What volume of the iceberg is above the water line?</u> Assume a <u>density for the saltwater ice of 0.920 kg/m$^3$</u> and a <u>saltwater density of 1.024 kg/m$^3$</u>.

As in the other example problems, the underlined material will become the basis of defining the variables and values.

- Step 2: Let us consider the concepts and principles involved in the problem. Here is a list of concepts that may be part of the problem:
    - Density
    - Volume
    - Buoyancy
    - Mass
    - Force
    - Weight

Here is a list of the principles, definitions, and laws that will be used:

- Archimedes' principle
- Newton's first law of motion
- Definition of density
- Definition of weight

This list will be the basis of the formation of the equations in step 6. Again, as stated in previous examples, when students become more comfortable with the process, this step may be eliminated.

- Step 3: Let's formulate the basic drawing for this problem (see Figure 5.6).

**FIGURE 5.6**

The Iceberg Problem

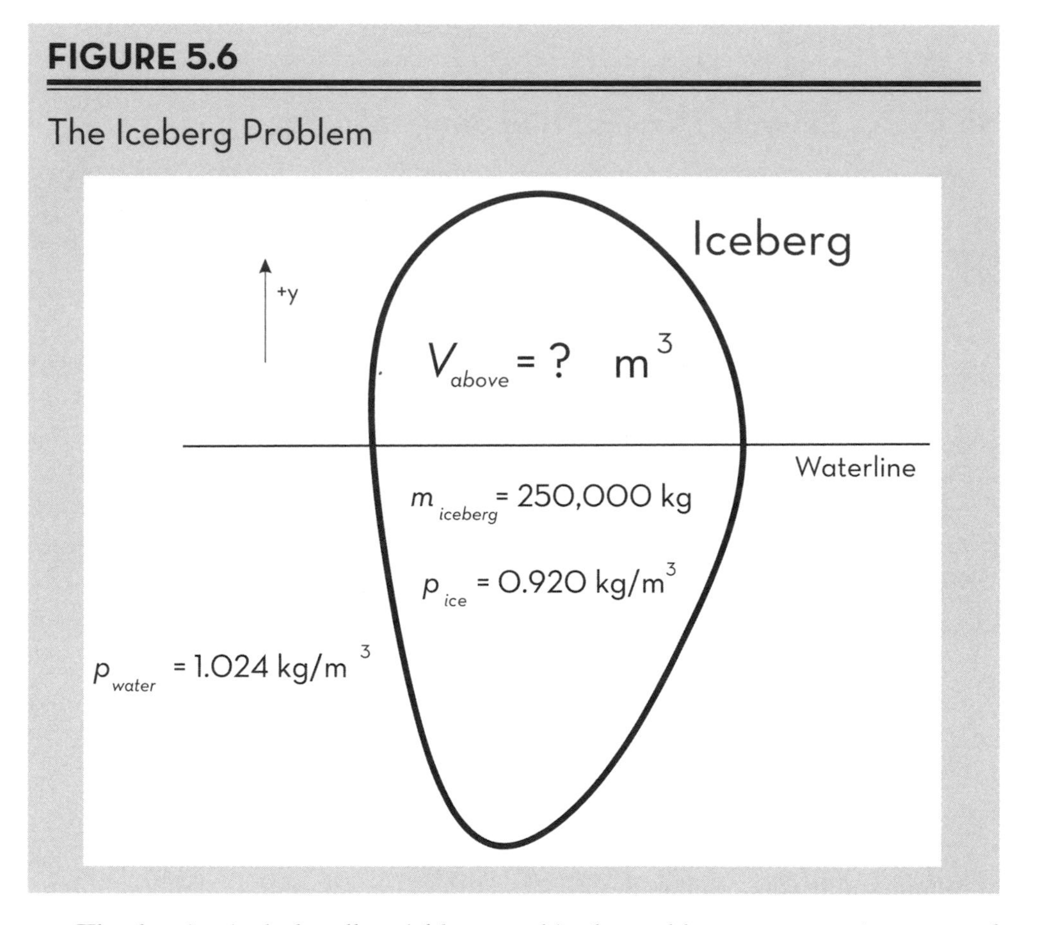


The drawing includes all variables stated in the problem statement, knowns and unknowns, with reasonable variable names, units, and numerical values for the knowns and a question mark for the unknown as required of this step. They are integrated into the drawing so they are in close proximity to the pertinent object or material. Furthermore, an axis has been placed in the drawing to define the direction of positive vectors. The student should be able to work the problem now without referring back to the written problem statement.

Just like in previous examples, this step allows for alterations to the drawing or for the formation of new drawings that assist in the process of extracting the equations from the principles. To apply Newton's first law for this problem, a free-body diagram is formed. It can be placed on the original drawing or formed as a new drawing as shown in Figure 5.7.

**FIGURE 5.7**

The Iceberg Problem Free-Body Diagram

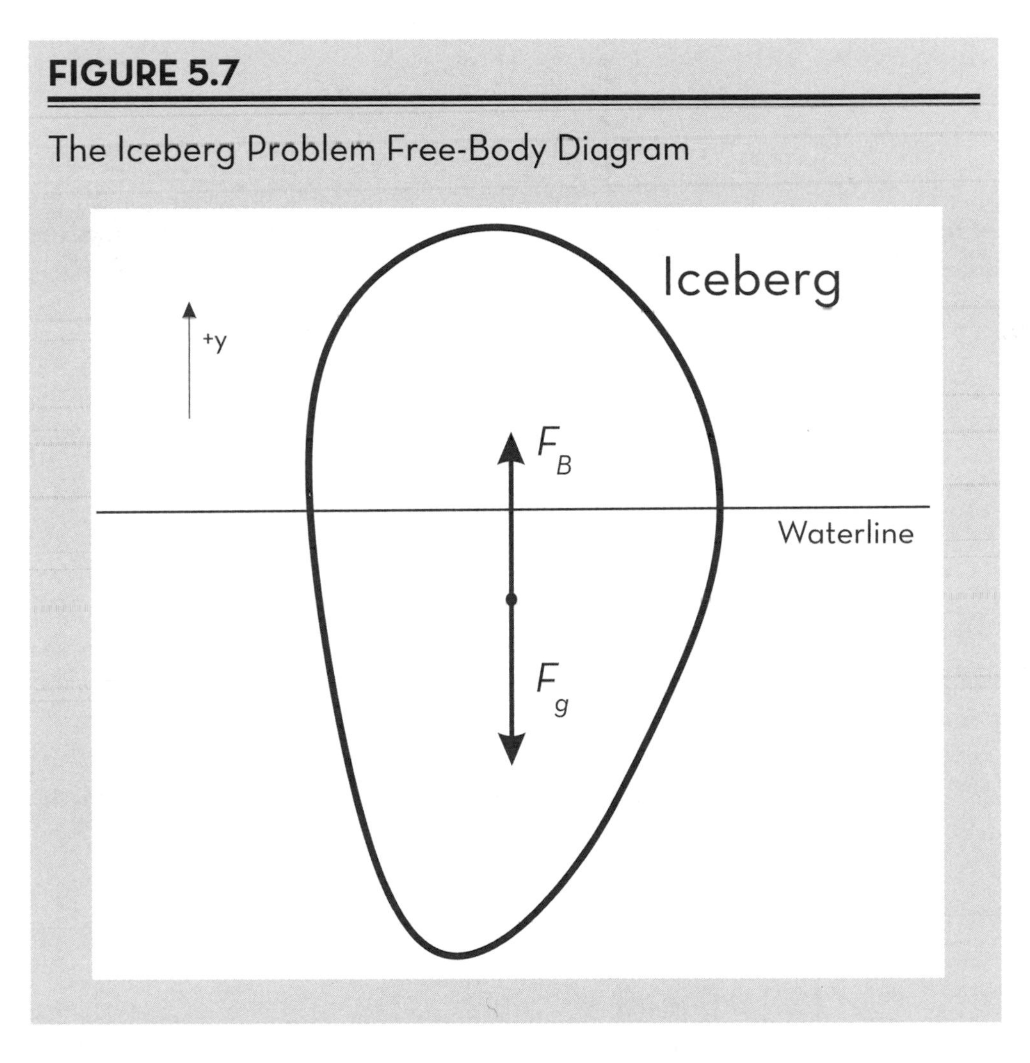


- Steps 4 and 5: These steps are skipped for this problem, as we are using a drawing. The knowns and unknowns are already integrated into the drawing.
- Step 6: Now we will list the equations, starting with an equation containing the unknown:

$$V_{above} = V_{total} - V_{below}$$

This is the definition of the volume above the water line in terms of the total volume ($V_{total}$) and the volume below the water line ($V_{below}$), both of which are connected to the principles in our list from step 2. Note that the equation is already solved for the unknown, so no algebraic manipulation is necessary for this equation. Now the equation is analyzed, placing a "?" on the unknown and a "√" on each known listed on the drawing:

$$\overset{?}{V}_{above} = V_{total} - V_{below} \qquad (1)$$

Note that there are no checked items because neither $V_{total}$ or $V_{below}$ appear as knowns in the drawing. These two variables are intermediate unknowns, and their existence implies the need for two more equations, one for each of the intermediate unknowns. These equations are formed in terms of other knowns in the drawing as much as possible:

$$\rho_{ice} = \frac{m_{iceberg}}{V_{total}}$$

$$F_B = \rho_{water} g V_{below}$$

In these equations, $g$ is the acceleration due to gravity, and $F_B$ is the buoyancy force (weight of the displaced water).

The first equation is the definition of density of the ice and the second is the definition of the buoyancy force—a definition that will be needed to apply Archimedes' principle listed in step 2.

Both of these equations need to be solved for the two intermediate unknowns, and a "?" is placed on the intermediate unknowns and a "√"on the knowns from the drawing:

$$\overset{?}{V}_{total} = \frac{\overset{\surd}{m}_{iceberg}}{\underset{\surd}{\rho_{ice}}} \qquad (2)$$

$$\overset{?}{V}_{below} = \frac{F_B}{\underset{\surd}{\rho_{water}}\underset{\surd}{g}} \qquad (3)$$

The first of the two equations has no new intermediate unknowns, so it is now ready for substitutions. The second of the two equations has one new intermediate unknown, $F_B$, which means that a new equation containing that variable must be formulated. The equation for that variable comes from the free-body diagram and Newton's first law of motion:

$$F_B - F_g = 0$$

Here, $F_g$ is the gravitational force on the iceberg. The axes chosen in the drawing determined that $F_B$ receives a positive sign and $F_g$ receives a negative sign in this vector component equation. This equation is solved for the intermediate unknown $F_B$ and a question mark is placed on $F_B$:

$$\overset{?}{F_B} = F_g \qquad (4)$$

$F_g$ is an intermediate unknown. Therefore, another equation must be formulated containing $F_g$, the definition of the gravitational force:

$$\overset{?}{F_g} = \overset{\surd}{m_{iceberg}}\overset{?}{g} \quad (5)$$

Note that this equation has no unmarked variables. When there are no new intermediate unknowns, we are sure we have enough equations for the solution. We now have the complete set of equations, (1) to (5), in the correct order of evaluation for the next step. Note that it is an option at this point to algebraically combine the equations. For problems in which the answer needs to be an expression, this is what should be done. Because this is a numerical problem, we will not do that here.

- Step 7: The equations of step 6 are now evaluated in reverse order, starting with equation (5) and working upward until the unknown in equation (1) has been evaluated. Specifically, as the numbers are inserted into the variables, the intermediate unknowns are calculated and then placed in the next equation of lower number:

$$F_g = m_{iceberg}\, g = (250{,}000\, kg)(9.8\, m/s^2) = 2.5\times10^6\, N \quad (5)$$

$$F_B = F_g = 2.5\times10^6\,\mathrm{N} \quad (4)$$

$$V_{below} = \frac{F_B}{\rho_{water}\, g} = \frac{2.5\times10^6\,\mathrm{N}}{(1.024\frac{kg}{m^3})(9.8\frac{m}{s^2})} = 2.5\times10^5 m^3 \quad (3)$$

$$V_{total} = \frac{m_{iceberg}}{\rho_{ice}} = \frac{250{,}000\, kg}{(0.920\frac{kg}{m^3})} = 2.7\times10^5 m^3 \quad (2)$$

$$V_{above} = V_{total} - V_{below} = (2.7\times10^5 m^3) - (2.5\times10^5 m^3)$$

$$= 2.0\times10^4\,\mathrm{m}^3 \qquad (1)$$

Note that numbers are substituted on paper with their units. Dimensional analysis is performed on each equation as a check. Remember that skipping this step deprives the problem solver of a good check of the equations before final evaluation with a calculator.

- Step 8: Now, the final answer is checked. We already know the units are correct. We must now determine if the answer makes sense.

It is well known that less than 10% of an iceberg is above the water line. If we divide our answer for the volume above the water line ($V_{above}$) by the total volume ($V_{total}$) and multiply by 100%, we get 8%, which agrees with the known measurements.

## *A Chemistry Example: Calculating Molarity*

Let's look at a problem that is not amenable to a drawing. This problem is typical of calculations that occur in chemistry where much of the laboratory calculations have no clear graphical interpretation. This example will demonstrate the strength of step 6 in the formulation of the equation set and how it leads to easy substitution of values for evaluation in step 7. The strength of step 8 in the checking of the answer will also be demonstrated. Let's state the problem: a calculation of molarity.

A mass of 4.5 mg of copper (II) sulfate is dissolved in water to produce 78 centiliters (cl) of solution. What is the molarity of the solution?

- Step 1: The first step says to read the problem over twice, the first time quickly and the second time actively. The second time through, the reader should highlight or underline important information to extract. It is recommended that this be done one sentence at a time. Here is an example of the problem read actively:

<u>A mass of 4.5 mg of copper (II) sulfate</u> is dissolved in water to produce <u>78 cl of solution</u>. <u>What is the molarity of the solution?</u>

The underlined material will become the basis of defining the variables and values.

- Step 2: Now is the time to think about the concepts and principles involved in solution of the problem. Here is a list of concepts that may be part of this problem's solution:
    - Solution, solute, solvent
    - Molarity

- Moles
- Molar mass

Here is a list of the principles, definitions, and laws that will be used:

- Equation for molarity
- Definition of moles
- Definition of molar mass
- Periodic table of the elements

This list will be the basis of the formation of the equations in step 6. As students become more comfortable with the process, this step may be eliminated.

- Step 3: As stated, there is no natural graphic representation of this problem that is useful for the solution, so this step (make a drawing) will be skipped.
- Steps 4 and 5: Using the active reading of step 1, we formulate two columns of variables:

| **Knowns** | **Unknowns** |
|---|---|
| $\text{mass}_{\text{sol}} = 4.5 \text{ mg}$ | $M = ?\ M$ |
| $V_{soln} = 78 \text{ cl } CuSO_4$ | |

The variable names are chosen according to conventions and are formed with just enough detail to ensure clarity without undue name length. Note that the values are written with correct significant figures and the given units. The unknown, the molarity, is marked with a "?"

- Step 6: Now, we will list the equations, starting with an equation containing the unknown:

$$M = \text{moles}_{\text{sol}} / V_{\text{soln}} (L)$$

This is the definition of the molarity in terms of the number of moles of solute ($CuSO_4$) and the volume of solution in liters. Note that this expression comes directly from the list of concepts and principles in step 2. Note also that the equation is already solved for the unknown, so no algebraic manipulation is necessary for this equation. Now the equation is analyzed, placing a "?" on the unknown and a "√" on each known listed on the drawing:

$$\overset{?}{M} = \text{moles}_{\text{sol}} / \overset{\surd}{V}_{\text{soln}} (L) \qquad (1)$$

Note that $moles_{sol}$ is unchecked because it does not appear on our lists of knowns or unknowns from step 4. The variable $moles_{sol}$ is an intermediate unknown, and its existence implies the need for another equation. This equation is formed in terms of other knowns in the drawing as much as possible.

$$moles_{sol} = mass_{sol}\,(1/mm)$$

The variable *mm* is the molar mass of $CuSO_4$. This equation is the definition of moles and is designated on our list of principles in step 2. Note that this equation requires no algebra because it is already solved for the intermediate unknown $moles_{sol}$. Let's analyze this equation using a "?" for the intermediate unknown and a "√" for the knowns in the equation:

$$\overset{?}{moles_{sol}} = \overset{\surd}{mass_{sol}}\,(1/mm) \qquad (2)$$

Note that the variable *mm*, which is not listed on the known or unknown lists, is unmarked, which implies the need for a new equation with *mm* as the intermediate unknown. We obtain this equation from the definition of molar mass and data from a periodic table (step 2):

$mm$ = sum of atomic masses for $CuSO_4$

In the equation, the atomic masses for Cu, S, and O will be taken directly from a periodic table and therefore may be treated as knowns. The equation is already solved for the intermediate unknown *mm*. Therefore, analysis of the equation with "?" and "√" symbols yields:

$\overset{?}{mm}$ = sum of $\overset{\surd}{\text{atomic}}$ masses for $CuSO_4$ (3)

Note that this equation has no unmarked variables. When there are no new intermediate unknowns, we are sure we have enough equations for the solution. We now have the complete set of equations (1), (2), and (3) in the correct order of evaluation for the next step. Note that it is an option at this point to algebraically combine the equations. For problems in which the answer needs to be an expression, this is what should be done. Since this is a numerical problem, we will not do that here.

- Step 7: The equations of step 6 are now evaluated in reverse order, starting with equation (3) and working upward until the unknown in equation (1) has been evaluated. Specifically, as the numbers are inserted into the variables of equation (3), the intermediate unknowns are calculated and then placed in the next equation of lower number (2). The process is repeated for equation (2) and then equation (1):

  $mm = 1 \times 63.546$ g/mole **Cu**

$+ 1 \times 32.065$ g/mole **S**

$+ 4 \times 15.9994$ g/mole **O**

$= 159.609$ g/mole (3)

$\text{moles}_{\text{sol}} = 0.0045 \text{ g} \times (1 \text{ mole}/159.609 \text{ g}) = 2.819 \times 10^{-5}$ moles (2)

$M = 2.819 \times 10^{-5}$ moles/78 cl

$= 2.819 \times 10^{-5}$ moles/0.78 L

$= \underline{3.61 \times 10^{-5} \text{ M}}$ (1)

Note that the numbers are substituted on paper with their units. Dimensional analysis is performed on each equation as a check, and we know that the unit *M* is defined as moles/liter. Note also that students try to skip this step, but teachers need to be adamant that numbers do not get entered into a calculator until substitution and dimensional analysis on paper are completed.

- Step 8: Now we check the answer. We have already demonstrated that the units work. What about the magnitude of the number? Does it make sense?

We expect the molarity to be small because a small mass is being placed in a relatively large body of solvent. This analysis based on reasonableness is one method for checking your answer. As students become more experienced, their sophistication in performing this step will increase.

## *A Geometry and Algebra Problem With a Mistake: The Area of an Octagon*

Let's formulate an algebraic geometry problem with an intentional mistake in the problem statement. We do this to demonstrate step 8 to its fullest extent. Here is the problem:

Calculate the area (in $cm^2$) of a regular octagon with sides of length 5.2 cm and a radius of 7.8 cm.

So what is the mistake in this problem statement? Well, the length of a side of a regular polygon is not independent of the radius. But let's work the problem as if we don't see this error and see if the process of The Method can catch the mistake.

- Step 1: First, read the problem over twice, the first time in a cursory fashion and the second time actively. During the second reading, the reader highlights or underlines important information to extract. Here is the problem read actively:

Calculate the area (in cm$^2$) of a regular octagon with sides of length 5.2 cm and a radius of 7.8 cm.

The underlined material will become the basis of defining the variables and their values.

- Step 2: Now is the time to think about the concepts and principles involved in solving the problem. Here is a list of concepts that may be part of this problem's solution:
  - Octagon, polygon
  - Area
  - Length
  - Radius
  - Altitude

  Here is a list of the principles, definitions, and laws that will be used:
  - Area of a polygon from triangle areas
  - Definition of an octagon
  - Area of a triangle
  - Construction of altitudes

  This list will be the basis of the formation of the equations in step 6.

- Step 3: The drawing is depicted in Figure 5.8. Note that the unknowns and knowns have been integrated into the drawing in close proximity to the associated object. The variable names are conventional and the numbers have the correct number of digits and given units.
- Steps 4 and 5: Because variable information has been integrated into the drawing (Figure 5.8), we can skip these two steps.
- Step 6: The first equation must contain the unknown $A$. It is given by this equation:

$$A = 8\,A_{\text{triangle}}$$

$A_{\text{triangle}}$ is the area of each of the eight triangles emanating from the center of the octagon, as shown in Figure 5.8. No algebra is needed since it is already solved for the unknown. Marking this equation yields the first equation of the solution set:

$$\overset{?}{A} = 8\,A_{\text{triangle}} \qquad (1)$$

$A_{\text{triangle}}$ is unmarked, so we need another equation for this variable. We use the equation for the area of a triangle given by the following:

**FIGURE 5.8**

Octagon Area Problem Drawing

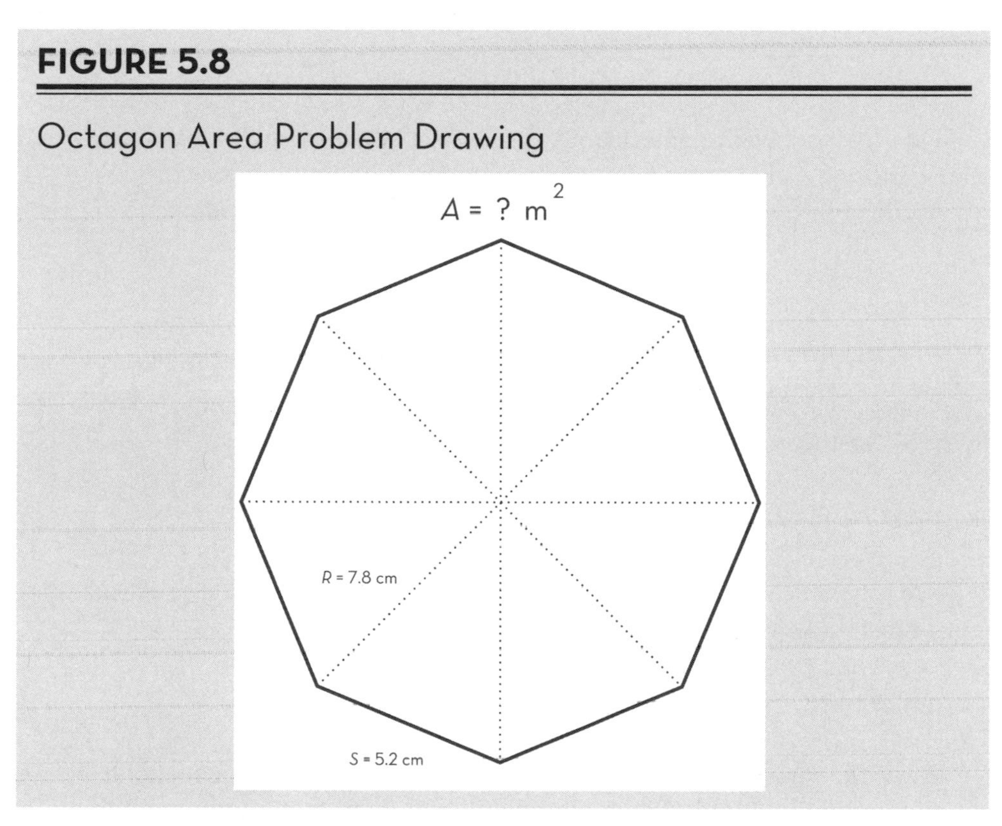


**FIGURE 5.9**

Octagon Area Problem Drawing With Altitude Construction

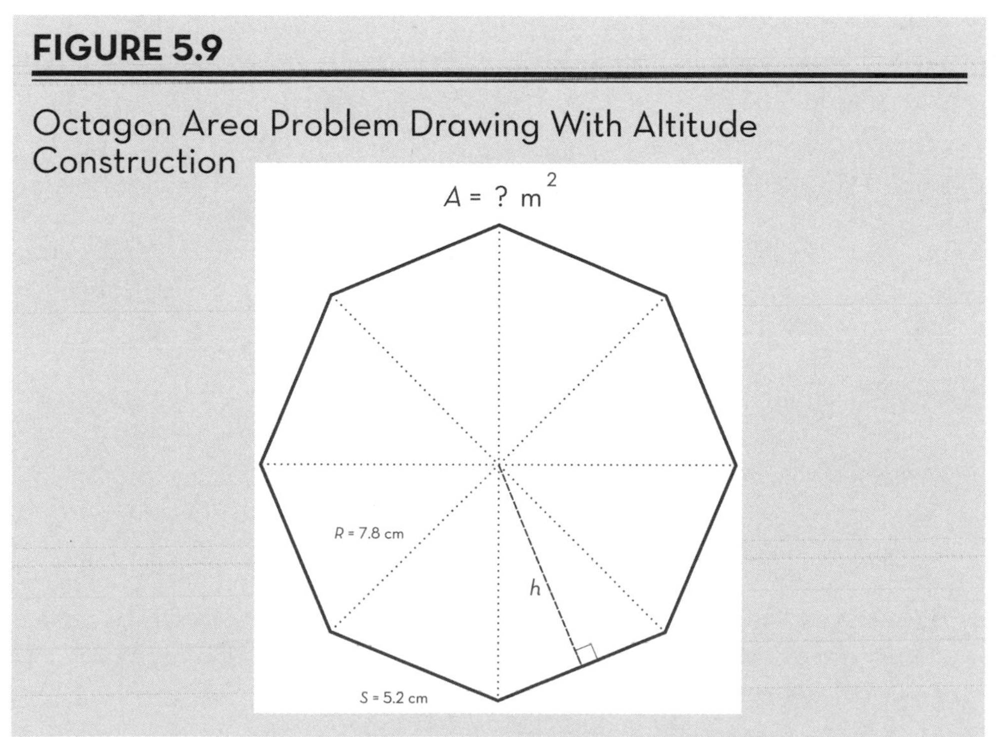

$A_{triangle} = \frac{1}{2} h\, S$

Here, $h$ is the height or altitude of a triangle as shown in the additional construction on the drawing as displayed in Figure 5.9 (p. 107).

Marking this equation yields the next equation in the solutions set:

$$\overset{?}{A}_{triangle} = \frac{1}{2} h\, \overset{?}{S} \qquad (2)$$

The variable $h$ is unmarked, so we need another equation containing $h$. We use the Pythagorean theorem from the construction in Figure 5.9:

$$h^2 + (S/2)^2 = R^2$$

We solve this equation for the variable $h$ and mark the equation to get the third equation of the solution set:

$$\overset{?}{h} = [\overset{\surd}{R}^2 - (\overset{\surd}{S}/2)^2]^{1/2} \qquad (3)$$

All of the variables of this equation are marked, so we now have the complete set of equations in the correct order.

- Step 7: Now we can evaluate these equations in reverse order to obtain the area of the octagon.

$$h = [(7.8 \text{ cm})^2 - (5.2 \text{ cm}/2)^2]^{1/2} \qquad (3)$$

$$= 7.4 \text{ cm}$$

$$A_{triangle} = \frac{1}{2} (7.4 \text{ cm})( 5.2 \text{ cm}) \qquad (2)$$

$$= 19.2 \text{ cm}^2$$

$$A = 8 \times (19.2 \text{ cm}^2) \qquad (1)$$

$$= \underline{154 \text{ cm}^2}$$

- Step 8: Now let us check this answer and observe why it can't possibly be correct. Observe the drawing in Figure 5.10 of our octagon circumscribed by a circle and inscribing a second smaller circle.

The area of the circumscribed circle is given by this expression:

$A_c = \pi R^2 = 191.13 \text{ cm}^2$

The area of the inscribed circle is given by this expression:

$A_i = \pi h^2 = 169.72 \text{ cm}^2$

According to Figure 5.10, the area of the octagon should be between these two values. It is not! At this point, a student can examine the problem and discover the fallacy in the problem statement. We know that the triangle's angle at the center of the octagon is 1/8 of 360°. This fixed angle means that the radius of the regular octagon is dependent on the length of the side and not independent.

We can see the importance of the check in step 8 and the sophistication this can sometimes require. Again, students will develop this sophistication with experience.

It should be stressed again that The Method is not a replacement for a comprehensive understanding of the concepts and principles; it is a systematic

**FIGURE 5.10**

Checking the Calculated Octagon Area Compared to Circumscribed and Inscribed Circle Areas

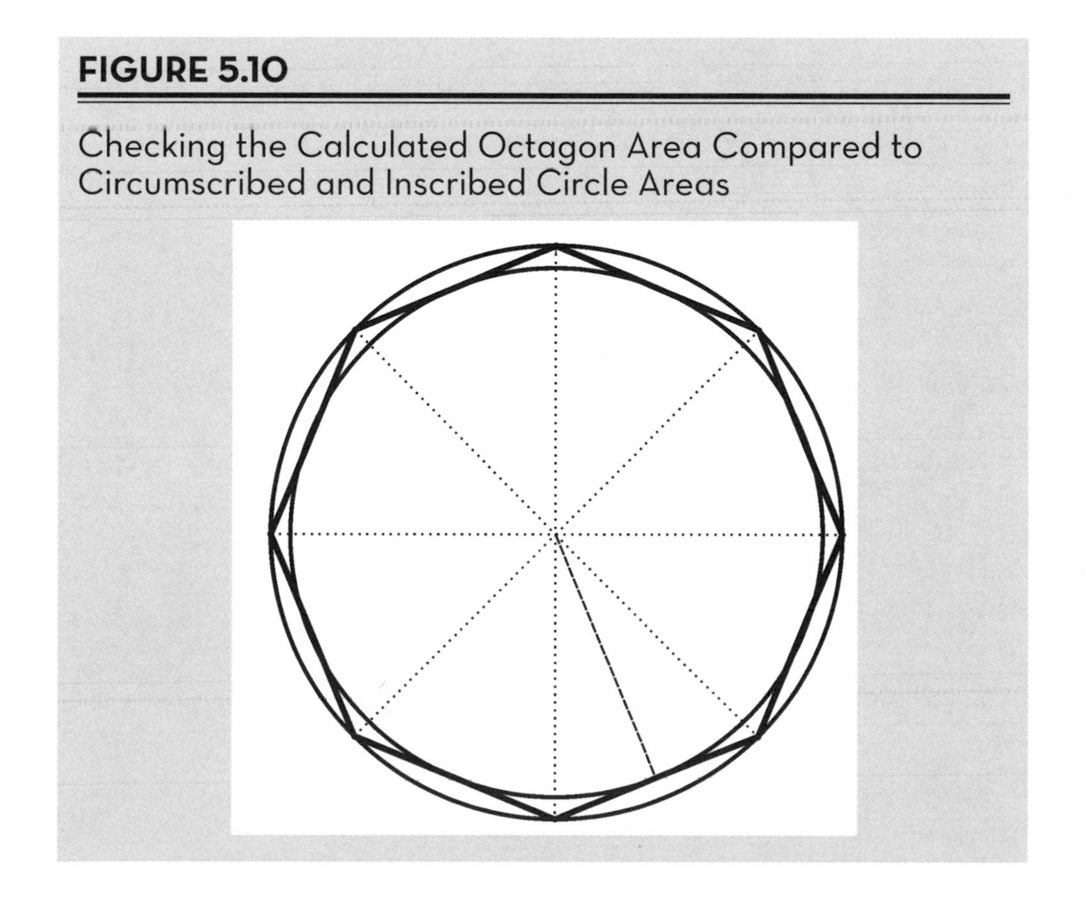

## FIGURE 5.11

Student Example of The Method

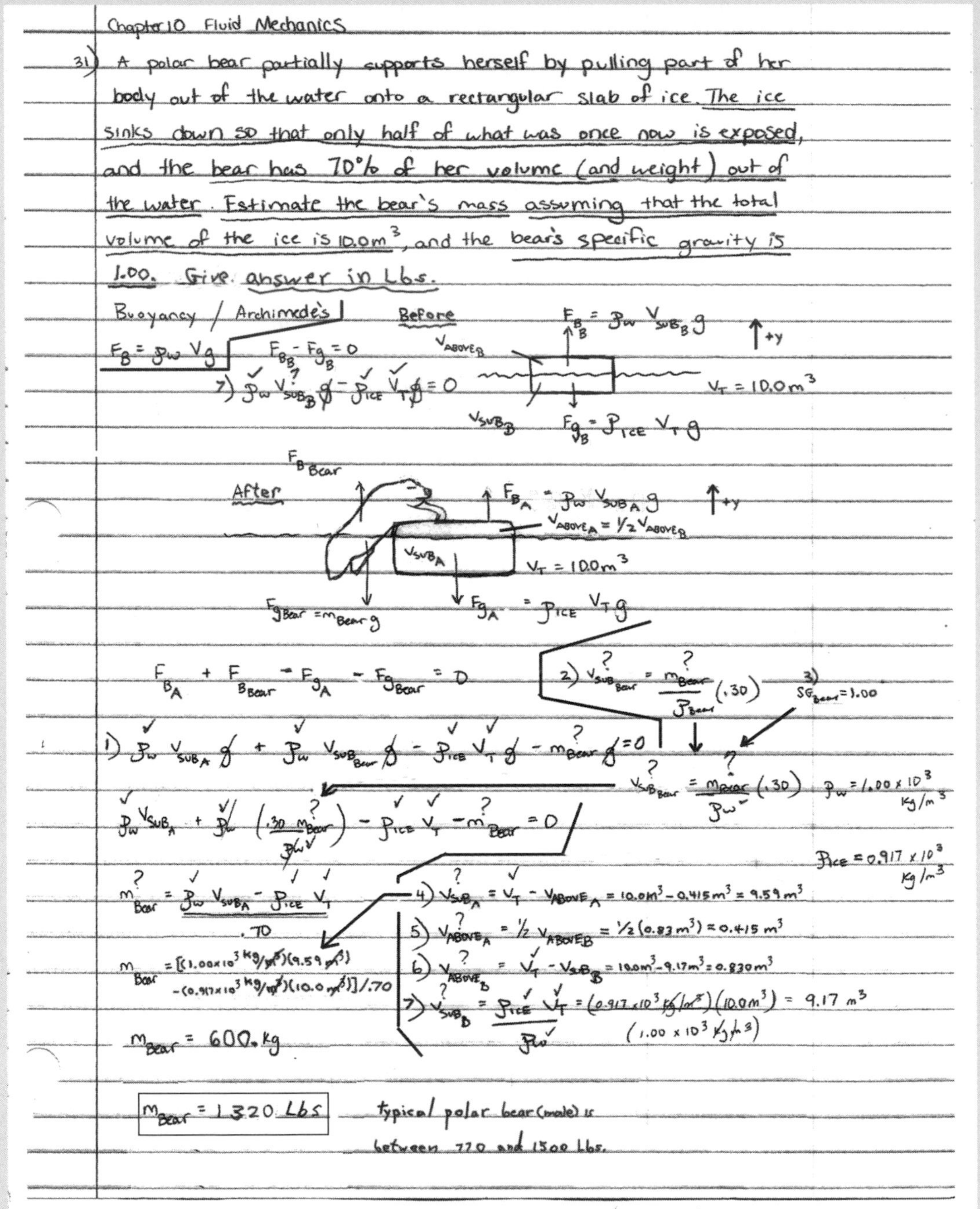

Chapter 10 Fluid Mechanics

31) A polar bear partially supports herself by pulling part of her body out of the water onto a rectangular slab of ice. The ice sinks down so that only half of what was once now is exposed, and the bear has 70% of her volume (and weight) out of the water. Estimate the bear's mass assuming that the total volume of the ice is $10.0\,m^3$, and the bear's specific gravity is 1.00. Give answer in Lbs.

Buoyancy / Archimede's

$F_B = \rho_w V g$

Before

$F_{B_B} - F_{g_B} = 0$

7) $\rho_w V_{SUB_B} g - \rho_{ICE} V_T g = 0$

$F_{B_B} = \rho_w V_{SUB_B} g$ ↑+y

$V_{ABOVE_B}$, $V_{SUB_B}$, $V_T = 10.0\,m^3$

$F_{g_B} = \rho_{ICE} V_T g$

After

$F_{B_{Bear}}$

$F_{B_A} = \rho_w V_{SUB_A} g$ ↑+y

$V_{ABOVE_A} = \frac{1}{2} V_{ABOVE_B}$

$V_{SUB_A}$, $V_T = 10.0\,m^3$

$F_{g_{Bear}} = m_{Bear} g$

$F_{g_A} = \rho_{ICE} V_T g$

$F_{B_A} + F_{B_{Bear}} - F_{g_A} - F_{g_{Bear}} = 0$

2) $V_{SUB_{Bear}} = \frac{m_{Bear}}{\rho_{Bear}}(.30)$

3) $SG_{Bear} = 1.00$

1) $\rho_w V_{SUB_A} g + \rho_w V_{SUB_{Bear}} g - \rho_{ICE} V_T g - m_{Bear} g = 0$

$V_{SUB_{Bear}} = \frac{m_{Bear}}{\rho_w}(.30)$

$\rho_w = 1.00 \times 10^3\ kg/m^3$

$\rho_w V_{SUB_A} + \rho_w \left(\frac{.30\, m_{Bear}}{\rho_w}\right) - \rho_{ICE} V_T - m_{Bear} = 0$

$\rho_{ICE} = 0.917 \times 10^3\ kg/m^3$

$m_{Bear} = \frac{\rho_w V_{SUB_A} - \rho_{ICE} V_T}{.70}$

4) $V_{SUB_A} = V_T - V_{ABOVE_A} = 10.0\,m^3 - 0.415\,m^3 = 9.59\,m^3$

5) $V_{ABOVE_A} = \frac{1}{2} V_{ABOVE_B} = \frac{1}{2}(0.83\,m^3) = 0.415\,m^3$

6) $V_{ABOVE_B} = V_T - V_{SUB_B} = 10.0\,m^3 - 9.17\,m^3 = 0.830\,m^3$

7) $V_{SUB_B} = \frac{\rho_{ICE} V_T}{\rho_w} = \frac{(0.917 \times 10^3\ kg/m^3)(10.0\,m^3)}{(1.00 \times 10^3\ kg/m^3)} = 9.17\,m^3$

$m_{Bear} = [(1.00 \times 10^3\ kg/m^3)(9.59\,m^3) - (0.917 \times 10^3\ kg/m^3)(10.0\,m^3)]/.70$

$m_{Bear} = 600.\ kg$

$m_{Bear} = 1320$ Lbs

typical polar bear (male) is between 770 and 1500 Lbs.

Figure 7.11 Student Example of The Method

approach to solving problems that includes good bookkeeping of variables and internal checks.

Figure 5.11 (p. 110) displays a student sample of a problem solved using The Method. A rubric for grading problem solving using The Method is given in Appendix F.

Teachers need to remind students that the real goal of The Method is to develop problem-solving skills for a lifetime. Students who learned the process with simple problems in high school are now applying it to complex problems in college and teaching the process to their fellow students and their professors. For this reason, learning The Method is as important for the advanced student as it is for those who struggle with problem solving.

## TABLE 5.1

### Subprocesses for Common Problem Types

| Problem Types | Subprocess |
|---|---|
| Solving single-equation algebra problems | 1. Use PEMDAS rules for order of operation.<br>2. Whatever is done to one side of an equation must be done exactly the same to the other side of the equation.<br>3. Undo functions with their inverse functions. |
| Solving systems of equations | 1. Use substitution method or elimination method. |
| Simple stoichiometry problems | 1. Convert quantity to moles using proper conversion factor (molar mass for grams, Avogadro's number for number of particles, 22.4 L/mole for gas at STP, ideal gas law for gas at other conditions).<br>2. Convert moles to moles of another compound using ratio from balanced chemical formula.<br>3. Convert moles to new quantity using one of the same conversion factors available in step 1. |
| Electron configuration counting | 1. Divide periodic table into s-block, p-block, d-block, and f-block.<br>2. Starting at hydrogen, count out the configuration using the row for the shell number, the blocks for the sublevel, and the number of columns in the block for the number of electrons in the sublevel. Go down one shell number when in a d-block and two shell numbers when in an f-block. |

**TABLE 5.1** *(continued)*

| Problem Types | Subprocess |
|---|---|
| Physics problems with two-dimensional vectors | 1. Take components of all vectors in the drawing along $x$ and $y$ and give their names $x$ and $y$ subscripts.<br>2. Break the problem into an $x$ and $y$ problem by splitting the vector equation into component equations in terms of the component names in the drawing. |
| Conservation law problems | 1. Draw a before-and-after picture for the process.<br>2. Calculate the conserved quantity for each drawing, before and after, and set them equal to each other. |
| Wave and resonance problems | 1. Convert resonator length to wavelength based on the fraction of the wave in the resonator as determined by fundamental or harmonic number.<br>2. Use $\lambda f = v$ to determine the corresponding frequency.<br>3. Use a musical interval to determine the new frequency.<br>4. Use $\lambda f = v$ to determine the corresponding wavelength.<br>5. Convert wavelength to resonator length based on fundamental or harmonic number.<br>Note: Not all steps will be necessary for all problems. |
| Optics ray tracing for mirrors | 1. Go from object to the mirror parallel to the center line and then through the focus.<br>2. Go from the object through the focus and then from the mirror parallel to the center line.<br>3. Image is where these two paths intersect.<br>Note: If the second part of each of these paths does not intersect, reverse them. |
| Optics ray tracing for lenses | 1. Go from object to the lens parallel to the center line and then through a focus (choose the focus on the opposite side for convex lenses and on the same side for concave lenses).<br>2. Go from the object through the other focus and then from the lens parallel to the center line.<br>3. Image is where these two paths intersect.<br>Note: If the second part of each of these paths does not intersect, reverse them. |
| Thermal equilibrium | 1. Set the heat lost by one substance equal to the negative of the heat gained by the other substance.<br>2. Substitute the expression $mC\,\Delta T$ with the appropriate variables for the heats.<br>3. Solve for the final temperature at equilibrium. |

**TABLE 5.1** *(continued)*

| Problem Types | Subprocess |
|---|---|
| First law of thermodynamics | 1. Model work, heat, and internal energy of a given thermodynamic process by examining a piston-cylinder model of the process or examining a heat sink model of the process.<br>2. Use the first law of thermodynamics to determine values. |
| Calculate the electric field (electric potential) at a point from a number of point charges | 1. Determine the electric field (electric potential) at the point from each of the charges using Coulomb's law (point charge electric potential equation) and direction rules.<br>2. Add the electric field (electric potential) values at the point as vectors (numbers). |
| Calculate the magnetic field at a point due to a number of current elements. | 1. Calculate the magnetic field at the point for each current element using the equation of the magnetic field due to a current at a distance. Use the right-hand rule to determine the direction.<br>2. Add the magnetic fields at the point together as vectors. |
| Calculate the electromotive force, current, and current direction in a conducting loop with a resistance in a changing magnetic flux. | 1. Use Faraday's law to calculate the electromotive force from the magnetic flux change rate.<br>2. Use Ohm's Law to calculate the magnitude of the current in the loop.<br>3. Use Lenz's Law to determine the direction of the current in the loop. |

## Subprocesses for Specific Problem Types

The Method is used for most problems. However, each problem type has its own subprocesses, often associated with going from the drawing to the equations—a subprocess within the general framework of The Method.

Table 5.1 (p.111) exhibits some common subprocesses from mathematics, chemistry, and physics. It is not exhaustive but demonstrates how these subprocesses can be used for given problem types. We applied the subprocess for two-dimensional vector problems for the inclined plane problem given earlier.

Students must comprehend that each type of problem has commonalities of processes and tools, and that those commonalities give structure to the subject matter to enhance understanding. They must also develop the ability to recognize problem types so that they may determine the appropriate subprocess to use.

# CHAPTER 6

# How to Analyze: Building the Perfect Laboratory Rat

Now that problem solving has been addressed, it is time to consider analytical thinking. Analysis includes any kind of investigation that involves the collection and analysis of data and the formulation of rational conclusions from the data.

Scientific investigations can involve laboratory work, fieldwork, or observation of phenomena. Many students are under the mistaken impression that all scientific investigations are performed by people in lab coats in laboratory facilities; however, the police detective investigating a crime scene or the zoologist observing the behavior of animals in the wild is also performing a scientific investigation.

For students getting their first taste of laboratory work, teachers often supply laboratory descriptions where the procedures are given to the student. On the advanced end, scientific investigations can involve the actual design and implementation of the investigation—both equipment and procedures.

Mastering analytical thinking is equally important to problem-solving proficiency for students' enrichment and their preparation for professional careers. Analytical thinking is one of the top three categories in Bloom's taxonomy, and mastery of it will provide an excellent foundation for a wide variety of professional tasks found in the work and school environments.

## Laboratory Mythology

There is a mythology that surrounds laboratory lessons that is incredibly prevalent in the teaching community. It started with the move toward student-centered, hands-on learning in schools. The benefits of this approach to learning are well documented, but lack of understanding of the subtleties of this new paradigm has caused this mythology to take root, to the detriment of real learning. Let's take a look at a few of these myths:

- *All students love doing laboratories.* If you talk to students, it becomes apparent that the assignment of laboratories often conjures fear and loathing for many of them. Why? Because students often find the advanced analytic thinking involved to be daunting, and they look at the resulting laboratory report as an unwelcome chore.

All students do not enjoy laboratories just because they are hands-on, despite what teachers may believe. There is no doubt that laboratories are crucial for attaining subject mastery; however, it is important that teachers discard this myth during the planning and execution of their lessons so that the needs of all students can be met effectively. By discarding this myth, teachers can mitigate some of the fear and loathing by streamlining the laboratories, using techniques such as asking probing questions, and relating the lab concepts to real-life processes that are familiar to students.

- *All laboratories are fascinating.* I have observed teachers doing a pre-lab lesson and expressing to their students just how fun and amazing the lab will be. The students then perform the laboratory the next day, only to be let down.
  There is nothing worse than overselling a laboratory to the students. We live in a world where our students are bombarded with technological marvels on a daily basis. They are rarely amazed or dazzled by the simple phenomena that happen in the typical high school laboratory. Teachers must not treat a lab as a source of entertainment, but as a tool for self-discovery. Treating it as such gives the laboratory educational value and challenges the students' thought processes and comprehension. Challenging the students with probing questions during the laboratory will keep the students engaged.
- *The entire course can be taught with a series of laboratories with no problem solving.* There are teachers who instruct their entire science course as one laboratory after another. They often state that this is the proper way to teach and students get everything they need from this approach. This is a grave mistake. Analytic thinking and problem solving are two parts of a whole in the sciences, and neither should be neglected. The laboratories should be viewed as a tool for developing an understanding of concepts and principles that are applied later to solve practical problems.

Note that I am not suggesting that laboratories are unimportant or should be eliminated in lesson planning; the converse is true. Teachers must be realistic, however, about the truths of students' thinking on these matters. Failure to do so can adversely affect learning.

## Scientific Method: Yeah, So What?

Most students are introduced to the "scientific method" before high school (see Figure 6.1). But in discussions with high school students, it becomes apparent that they often have little conceptual understanding of the true importance or purpose of the scientific method. Teachers often present the scientific method as a series of sections that must be in the lab reports for students to get full credit during assessment. This situation is unfortunate, as it leads to naive conceptions.

Students need to understand the scientific method as a process for conducting an investigation that leads to discovery of new information and relationships. They need to comprehend it as scaffolding for all types of investigative tasks. Furthermore, they need to appreciate it as a framework for attaining the higher-order thought processes required of collegiate and professional investigative environments.

**FIGURE 6.1**

Scientific Method

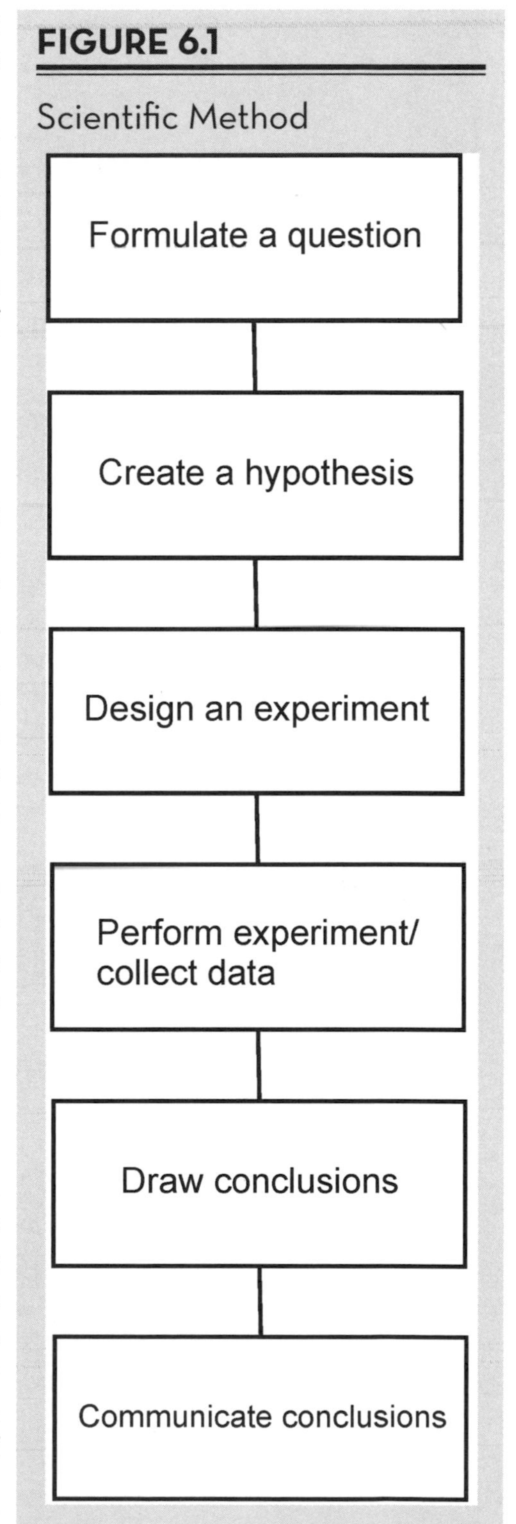


## So Why Are You Doing This Lab?

Teachers often assume students know why they are doing laboratory investigations in class. It is a fascinating, enlightening, and perplexing exercise to ask students why they do labs. When a group of senior high school students, who had been through a minimum of three lab-based classes, were asked this question, the most common responses were "Because the teacher made me do it," "Because it helps me understand science better," or "I have no idea." It becomes clear from a poll like this that students often do not understand the general reason why they do labs.

This lack of understanding of the purpose often leads to lab reports that read as if the students are desperate to grasp anything relevant in their data. Without knowing the target of the lab, the conclusion statements read as if the student is floundering for a way to write anything to fill paper.

### *"We Perform Laboratories to Discover or Verify Values, Trends, or Relationships."*

This is the reason labs are performed not just by students, but by professional scientists, too. This statement needs to be stressed as often as possible as students do laboratories in school. Understanding this statement gives the students a framework for successfully executing the formulation of a purpose statement and hypothesis for a specific laboratory task. It also provides a road map for laboratory design and implementation and guides the proper extraction of conclusions from their data analysis.

Most secondary school laboratories are performed to find

a numerical value for a parameter (e.g., the speed of sound in air) or a relationship between variables (e.g., the relationship between magnetic fields and current through a wire). By stressing this to the students on a regular basis, teachers provide a basic key to help students view laboratories in the proper light and produce better laboratory reports for assessment.

### *Labs In, Tools Out!*

Just like postulates and theorems in mathematics provide the tools for calculation of specific math problems, the numbers and relationships that are discovered or verified in laboratories provide the tools for problem solving in the sciences.

As was stated at the beginning of Chapter 4, understanding concepts and relationships is critical to success in problem solving. Laboratory investigations provide discovery and true comprehension of these concepts and relationships, dispelling naive conceptions and illuminating subtleties that are not so apparent in the resulting equations presented by traditional lecture approaches. This fits in well with the Exploration stage of the 5E learning cycle and the first stage of the Modeling Instruction cycle (Chapter 3), where laboratory investigations are used to discover concepts and principles and integrate them with prior knowledge. This is in contrast with the traditional method of using laboratories merely to confirm concepts and principles found and explained in textbooks. Students should be encouraged to perform laboratory design before the execution of the laboratory, and the results should be explored in a class discussion to extract concepts and principles . Further investigations through new laboratory investigations or demonstrations may be performed to learn to apply these new concepts and principles and extend comprehension.

## The Processes of Being a Good Rat

There is a set of behaviors and practices that teachers must encourage in their students for them to become proficient in a laboratory environment and comprehend the results of their investigations. In this section, we will look at these in some detail.

### *Understanding and Applying Good Rat Practices*

#### Asking the Right Questions

To formulate a good purpose statement and design a good laboratory procedure, students must have a good idea of the questions they will attempt to answer in the investigation. This is not always an easy thing to do, especially if the students are asked to design the laboratory procedures themselves, as is done in advanced laboratories to promote higher-order thinking. Teachers should have a pre-lab discussion with the students and ask probing questions to assist the students in the formulation of these questions and the creation of the resulting laboratory design.

### Applying the Right Processes

Even though most high school laboratories are fairly simple and straightforward, students need to understand what real laboratory scientists do when conducting a professional lab investigation. Scientists treat lab procedures as fluid, often modifying the procedures to reduce systematic errors or promote improved precision. These modifications could include changes in hardware or tweaks of the processes.

Teachers should encourage students to practice the same processes at some point in their lab assignments. As systematic errors occur, teachers can challenge the students to find methods to eliminate or reduce errors. This is an excellent way to promote good habits and mimic the processes students might need to consider in their careers. Note that any procedural changes should be recorded in the laboratory book for inclusion in the procedure section of the report.

### Safety, People!

An even more critical responsibility than teaching students how to conduct laboratory exercises is to send them home in the same physical condition in which they came to school. Teachers should stress safety in each and every laboratory that is executed. It is recommended that teachers point out especially dangerous aspects of a given laboratory and make students discuss mitigation procedures as part of the prelab write-up. A short review of these procedures should be conducted before the laboratory exercise is performed. In addition, teachers should perform constant monitoring of laboratory execution so dangerous situations can be avoided.

## Three Parts of Every Number

Unlike mathematics classes, the numbers in science problems often represent real, measured quantities. As such, the information pertaining to the type of variable that was measured and its precision must be an integral part of the number and propagated through any calculations performed. Teachers of science need to stress this constantly with their students, as mistakes or omissions with units and significant digits is one of the most common errors that students make.

Every number represented in a laboratory or calculation must have significant digits and units set by the measuring device used to produce it. If the numbers are given in a word problem, the significant digits and units are set in the problem statement and should be propagated through using the rules for significant digit manipulation:

- *Measured quantities versus defined quantities:* Measured quantities must have the number of significant digits determined by the measuring device. This is usually determined as the lowest increment on the measuring device (plus one guess digit if the measurement is taken by an analog device). Defined quantities such as constants are treated as having an infinite number of significant figures.

- *Counting significant digits of a number:* Here are the rules for counting significant digits of a number:
  1. All nonzero digits of the number are significant.
     Example: The number 237 has three significant digits.
  2. All zeroes of the number that are between two nonzero digits are significant.
     Example 1: The number 2008 has four significant digits.
     Example 2: The number 20.08 has four significant digits.
  3. All leftmost zeroes in the number are insignificant (placeholders).
     Example 1: The number 0053407 has five significant digits.
     Example 2: The number 0.0069 has two significant digits.
  4. All rightmost zeroes are significant if the number contains a decimal point; otherwise, they are insignificant (placeholders).
     Example 1: The number 0.04200 has four significant digits.
     Example 2: The number 3100 has two significant digits.
     Example 3: The number 3100. has four significant digits.
     Example 4: The number 3100.0 has five significant digits.
  5. Numbers used for counting (integers) and number definitions are treated as having an infinite number of significant digits.
     Example: 27 cats has an infinite number of significant digits
     Example: 1 foot = 12 inches has an infinite number of significant digits.
  6. For scientific notation numbers, the counting is performed on the nonexponent part of the number alone.
     Example: The number $2.53 \times 10^{-5}$ has three significant digits.
- *Multiplying and dividing numbers with correct significant digits:* The answer must have the same number of significant digits as the number with the least number of significant digits in the calculation. For example, let's multiply 3.492 N by 2.3 m:

  $$3.492 \text{ N} \times 2.3 \text{ m} = 8.0 \text{ Nm}$$

The number 2.3 m has two significant digits and the number 3.492 N has four significant digits. According to the rule, the answer must have two significant digits. That is why the answer is rounded to 8.0 Nm.

- *Adding and subtracting with correct significant digits:* The answer must have the same number of decimal places as the number with the least number of decimal places in the calculation. For example, let's subtract 4.372 m from 8.91 m:

  $$8.91 \text{ m} - 4.372 \text{ m} = 4.54 \text{ m}$$

The number 8.91 m has two decimal places and the number 4.372 m has three decimal places. According to the rule, the answer must have two decimal places, so the answer is rounded to 4.54 m.

- *Rounding numbers:* The usual rules for rounding numbers apply with digits of 4 or lower rounded down to 0 and digits of 5 or higher rounded up to 10.

## Two Measurements Are Better Than One. Three Is Even Better. Four? Even Better!

One aspect of laboratory work that often gets lost in the high school classroom is the statistical aspect. In real laboratory work, each measurement is usually made many times. A data point in a table or on a graph represents the mean of these repeated measurements and is usually accompanied by error bars representing the spread in the measurement data (standard deviation). This is one way that statistical error in measurements is mitigated, the other way being the taking of more data points for the graph and improving the line fit.

Because of limited classroom time in high school courses, it is usually not feasible for many measurements to be made for any laboratory. Still, this is an important aspect of laboratories that students should understand before they go to college. It is recommended that teachers take the time to do at least one laboratory in which the students are exposed to this statistical aspect of laboratories. Even students going into non-science-related fields should have an understanding of the importance of multiple measurements in increasing confidence levels in data sets. The concept comes up in a variety of professional tasks.

## The Processes of Data Presentation and Analysis

There are an alarming number of students who come to believe graphs are only for the presentation of data. They fail to comprehend the graph as a tool in data analysis—a tool equally as important as any symbolic mathematical manipulation that is performed. Constructing a graph from a data table can illuminate relationships in the data that are not as transparent when in table form. In addition, artifacts in the graph often provide key information for the determination of important parameters that fix the exact form of the relationship. Teachers need to be aware of this tendency to devalue graphs and guard against it in their laboratory lessons.

### *Making Proper Tables and Graphs*

In this section, we will discuss the proper way to construct graphs and tables for reports. Tables and graphs are central constructs for data presentation and analysis, making proper construction crucial to the analytical process.

#### Constructing Data Tables

Data tables should have the following elements when constructed for a report:

- *Descriptive title:* Avoid titles like "Table." Tables should have titles that are clear and unambiguous.

- *Clear presentation of correlations:* Several variables may be presented on a single table. The relationship between these variables should be clear to the reader from the placement on the table.
- *Labeled columns and rows, including units:* Labels should be descriptive and unambiguous. Units need not be placed on every number if the units are included on the column and row labels.
- *Correct numbers of significant digits for displayed values:* Again, significant digits are an important attribute of a laboratory number, as they display the precision of the measuring devices used.

## Constructing Graphs

Graphs should have the following elements when constructed for a report:

- *Size:* When possible, graphs should fill a whole page. This allows for more resolution, which leads to precise reading for analysis tasks.
- *Title:* The title should be descriptive of what is presented in the graph. Avoid vague or misleading titles that might cause the graph to be misinterpreted by the reader. Never title your graph "graph."
- *Labeled axes:* Each axis should have a complete description of the variable and the units. The independent variable (the one controlled by the experimenter) is displayed on the horizontal ($x$) axis and the dependent variable is displayed on the vertical ($y$) axis. Dual scales are sometimes used for the axes with the goal of looking at different units or multiple relationships.
- *Labeled scales:* Scales need to be chosen for each axis such that the data set fits within the grid of the graph but spreads across both axes as much as possible. Scales with divisions in 1s, 2s, 4s, 5s, 8s, and 10s (and multiples of 10) are common. Other choices make the graph difficult to interpret between scale divisions. If dual scales are used, divisions for both sets of units should be on the axes.
- *Symbols for data points:* Point symbols should be chosen such that a line does not obscure them if it passes through the point and so that they have well-defined centers. Common symbols include plus signs, $x$'s, bull's-eyes, squares, and asterisks. Never use dots for the points as they may be obscured by a line. When multiple lines are graphed on the same grid, different symbols for each graph may be used, with a legend to tell the reader what each symbol represents.
- *Lines:* Lines should be drawn neatly through the data. Lines may be fitted by tracing the line through the points such that each point is given sufficient influence (approximately same distance to the line and about the same number of points above and below the line). Alternatively, regression techniques may be applied that use statistics to do the best fit. The appropriateness of a given function in fitting a data set may also be determined using analytic techniques (chi-square calculation, for instance). If multiple lines are placed on the same grid, colors

or different dash patterns may be used with a legend to identify what each line represents. (Note: It is rarely a good idea to place more than five lines on the same graph, as confusion in reading and interpretation can result.)

- *Error bars:* Error bars represent the precision (standard deviation) of many measurements of the same data point. They are normally centered on the average value of all the measurements, with the length of the error bar set by the tolerance (standard deviation) of the measurements. They are commonly given for the dependent variable, but also can be given for the independent variable.

## Reading Tables and Graphs

Teachers can help students extract information from tables and graphs by teaching them what questions to ask when examining the table or graph. These questions provide scaffolding for performing efficient analysis of the data and extracting meaningful conclusions.

### Reading Tables

The following questions should be asked when reading a data table:

- *What does the title mean?* The title is your first and best clue for knowing how to interpret and read the table.
- *What do the labels on columns and rows mean?* These labels give the next clues as to the significance of the table.
- *What is the purpose of the table?* Understanding the importance of the data table within the context of a report is important to assessing purpose and significance.
- *Is there any significance to the mean, mode, or median of the data?* Sometimes these values have significance in the analysis.
- *Are there any maxima and minima in the data?* What would these extreme points mean?
- *Can you graph the data?* Create a graph if possible. This is the most important tool for analyzing the data, as it will illuminate relationships better than any other method.
- *Are there any important trends (increasing or decreasing) in the data?* These trends provide rough ideas as to the relationships that may exist in the data.

### Reading Graphs

The following questions should be asked when reading a graph and attempting to extract information during data analysis:

- *What does the title mean?* The title is your first and best clue as to the significance and importance of the graph.

- *What do the axis labels mean?* After evaluating the title, an examination of the axis labels provides more clues as to how to read and use the graph for analysis.
- *What are the domain and range?* The domain and range are given roughly by the scales of the graph (if the author did a good job picking the scales). The domain and range provide evidence of the regime of validity of the graph and, possibly, where the next phase of laboratory work needs to be concentrated.
- *What are the trends (increasing and decreasing) in segments of the domain, and what do they mean?* Sometimes, the domain can be broken down into sections that have distinct functional behaviors. The trends in these sections may provide keys to extracting important relationships and parameters.
- *What are the roots (*x *values at* y = 0*), and what do they mean?* The roots are the third most important aspect of most graphs. The $x$ values often have important meaning in the context of the investigation.
- *What is the* y*-intercept, and what does it mean?* This is the second most important parameter that can be extracted from a graph. It is often associated with equation constants and initial values.
- *What is the slope (linear graph only), and what does it mean?* Most graphs in high school labs are either linear or can be made linear. When a linear graph is produced, the student should automatically examine the slope and $y$-intercept and interpret these numbers. Slopes are often the most important parameters that can be calculated from these graphs. Note that they can be interpreted as rates for graphs when time is on the $x$-axis.
- *Where and what value are the maxima, minima, and saddle points, and what do they mean?* Extrema often have physical meanings on a graph. Deciding the meaning of these points (using the scale labels) can provide clues into the relationships and parameters of the equations that govern the data.
- *Where are the asymptotes located, and what do they mean?* As with the extrema, the asymptotes provide artifacts in the graph that can be used to set important parameters and define relationships (such as rational expressions).
- *What equation can be fitted to the graph, and to what accuracy?* Modern technology provides software tools for calculators and computers for the fast and accurate fitting of graphs to functions, including tools to tell whether the fit is appropriate. Teachers need to give their students opportunities to learn to use these tools in the context of their laboratory analysis.
- *Can the graph be transformed to linear?* As was stated earlier, many relationships can be made linear by a proper choice of function to transform either the $x$-variables, $y$-variables, or both. The transformations, along with the linear analysis, can illuminate the functional form of the relationship. For instance, a quadratic graph can be made linear by using the square of the variable on the $y$-axis instead of the variable itself.
- What are the amplitude, frequency, period, and phase (periodic graphs only)?

## Conclusions From the Data

Conclusions are one of the most difficult concepts for some students to grasp. Over the years, I have had some amazingly erroneous (and humorous) conclusions come to me in laboratory reports.

To understand what needs to be in a conclusion, it is often insightful to understand what should not be in a conclusion.

- Conclusions should never have opinions. The teacher doesn't need to hear how much the student enjoyed or hated the lab, how important or trivial the lab is, or that the student learned so much or not very much doing the lab. Conclusions are analytical, not evaluative. Indeed, conclusions should be written in third person. *I* and *me* have no place in a conclusion.
- Conclusions should never ramble. Extracted parameters and relationships should be stated succinctly.
- Conclusions are not a forum for complimenting (or insulting) the teacher. Regardless of the sincerity of the sentiment, it has no place in a conclusion.

### *Get to the Point!*

As stated above, being succinct and direct is proper for a conclusion. Being too wordy will just confuse the reader. Properly written, a lab report should be self-contained and give the reader a clear idea of the purpose of the investigation and what was found.

### *What Did I Do Wrong? Error Analysis*

Conclusions should contain an analysis of any observed systematic errors in the execution of the laboratory procedure, with statements of the effect on the captured data. This information gives the experimenter and the reader a basis for discussions of improvements of the procedure and equipment used.

### *How Could I Make the Procedure Better?*

Important aspects of analytic thinking that sometimes are given less emphasis than they should are procedural design and modification. Professional laboratory scientists, engineers, and technicians spend a significant amount of time on laboratory design and modifications to increase confidence in their results. Even in cases where the procedure is given to the students upfront, the students should be encouraged to consider how they can eliminate the delineated systematic errors by modification of the procedures. The students should state these modifications and their rationale in the conclusion.

# CHAPTER 6

## The Laboratory Report

### *Preparation for the Execution of a Laboratory*

There is nothing that can derail a laboratory exercise faster than students attempting the laboratory work when they are unprepared. As discussed previously, knowing the specific purpose of a given laboratory is essential to performing the laboratory correctly and making reasonable conclusions afterward.

Prelaboratory work should be conducted in two steps:

1. *Class discussion:* Teachers should lead students in a discussion of the laboratory the day before it is executed. The discussion should address the following points:
   - *Purpose:* As stated earlier, knowing the purpose of a laboratory is crucial to properly conducting the laboratory work and drawing accurate conclusions. Letting the students discuss their understanding of the purpose with their lab partners, with guidance from the instructor, is an excellent approach to ensuring student understanding of goals.
   - *Procedure:* A detailed discussion of the procedure for the laboratory work should be conducted. If the laboratory procedure is being designed by the students, teachers should review preliminary designs (possibly over a period of a few days) and assist the students in streamlining and correcting the steps as they work toward a final product for execution.
   - *Safety:* Major sources of physical risk due to equipment, materials, or procedures should be discussed, with emphasis on avoidance. Students should take notes that will become part of their laboratory procedures. This may include a summary of Material Safety Data Sheets (MSDS) and a statement of proper operation requirements from equipment manuals.

2. *Prelaboratory report.* The title, purpose, background, hypothesis, materials, procedure, and empty data tables of a laboratory report, discussed in the next section, should be written by the students prior to the conduct of the laboratory. This exercise ensures that the prelaboratory discussions are effective and students are truly ready to conduct the laboratory. Teachers should assess the prelaboratory documents before the laboratory is conducted and include this assessment as part of the grading rubric for the laboratory.

   Because of safety considerations, teachers should insist that the prelaboratory document be completed before the actual laboratory work is executed.

### *Template for a Laboratory Report*

Here is a template for producing a good professional-quality laboratory report. Students should be given this template at the beginning of the course and encouraged to use it in when writing their reports.

- *Title:* The title should be descriptive of the laboratory being done (e.g., "Measurement of Density of Solids").
- *Background:* The background is a presentation of prior knowledge or research done by the student presented as expositive text.
- *Purpose:* Why am I doing this lab? ("Because the instructor wants me to" is not a valid purpose.) Students should be specific about what they hope to measure or discover. Remember, labs are always about either measuring or verifying a specific quantity or quantities, or discovering or verifying relationships. State the purpose accordingly.
- *Hypothesis:* This can be an "if ... then" statement—an educated guess about what the results will look like. It can be based on prior knowledge or research. It is OK to guess wrong, but the students need to state that in the conclusion.
- *Materials:* Create a complete list of all equipment used in a laboratory. Students should not include things like the papers or pencils they are using to record data unless they are using these items to do the lab explicitly (e.g., pencil used as a pointer on a meterstick). Be descriptive with the individual items. For example, if a 50 ml beaker is used, say it is a 50 ml beaker. If a flask is used, state whether it is a Florence or Erlenmeyer flask, and state the volume.
- *Procedure:* This should include a complete and thorough listing of the steps used to perform the lab. This can and should include any steps the students added to improve the procedure during the lab execution. The steps should be numbered. If the procedure is in multiple parts, there should be multiple procedures. The heading for the procedure parts can be bulleted or lettered, but must include a descriptive heading telling the reader what the procedure part is for specifically. The steps within each procedure part are then numbered separately. Students may use an outline form. Safety instructions should be included in the procedure. *Data analysis:* This section includes measured data, graphs, and calculations. Data should be presented in table form when possible. Most often, the data will need to be graphed too. Calculations should be written out with words describing what is being done and why. They should be written using proper propagation of significant figures and units throughout the calculation. Scientific notation should be used for any extremely large or small numbers.
- *Follow-up questions:* These questions will test the students' understanding of the discovered relationships and see if they can extend the concepts and relationships to other cases. The questions as well as the answers should be written.

- *Conclusion:* This section states whether the students satisfied the purpose and the hypothesis. It should also present the values of any measured quantities and the mathematical or descriptive (trends, qualitative relationships) form of any discovered relationships. It should also include a good description of any known systematic errors and what effect they might have had on the result. Finally, description of procedure and equipment modifications for follow-up investigations may be stated.

  A rubric for grading laboratory reports is given in Appendix G.

## Rat Engineering: The Importance of Projects

Students love creativity. Even high school students love to draw, paint, sing, or dance, much like their younger peers. Those same students who must be constantly prodded to get work done in your science or math class can be found singing arias like a diva in choral class or painting like Dali in art class. Why is it so hard to motivate these students in an academic classroom? The reason is simple: Math and science classes are often devoid of opportunities to apply creativity. In the process of teaching students the basics of problem-solving skills and analytical thinking, the joy and beauty of the subject are often lost in the details. This is one area in which the language arts and social studies teachers have a distinct advantage. They have easy avenues for creativity that they can use in teaching the basics of their subjects. For the creative mind, it is necessary to find the creative side of mathematics and science and allow students a mechanism for exploring it. This creative aspect of science and mathematics is called engineering.

Teachers often mistakenly believe that laboratory explorations act as an inspiration source; however, a simple observation of students during laboratories demonstrates that many students don't find the needed inspiration in the execution of labs. Laboratories, as normally conducted, are analytical for the most part, not creative. Engineering projects, in contrast, require a creative approach.

One major engineering task is to apply physical principles and mathematical tools to create working products. These products could be mechanical, electrical, or chemical. Often, the design of the device starts with a set of requirements that bound the problem and the resulting characteristics of the product. The process requires both analytical skills and creativity for successful completion. It is this aspect of engineering that needs to be captured in lessons.

So, how can this be accomplished? Here are a couple of options:

- *Lab design:* Teachers can give their students a parameter to measure or a relationship to explore, but make it part of the laboratory assignment to assemble appropriate equipment and design the lab procedures themselves. Students can be given access to the equipment stockroom so that they can pick equipment to use in their design.

This type of laboratory combines analytical thinking with creativity. It requires the students to do research on equipment and capabilities as they assemble the apparatus and formulate the laboratory processes. This can be a daunting task for students who are used to canned laboratories. Teachers need to provide plenty of time and some guidance during the formulation of the lab design; however, this kind of laboratory can be quite exciting as students find different approaches to the same goal.

- *Engineering a device:* Give the students some specifications for the operation of a device (e.g., a device that causes a light to blink at a variable rate), and ask them to construct the device from equipment in the stockroom.

  With both approaches, it is vitally important to give the students plenty of guidance and encouragement without overinfluencing the creative process. It is prudent to have the students present a number of progress reports so the teacher can make suggestions and circumvent approaches that would take substantial time and lead to negative results. Given the increased challenge of this type of project, some flexibility of schedule may be necessary. Teachers must make sure that there is adequate availability of equipment in the stockroom to allow for successful completion of the project.

Initially, students can find this style of project to be quite overwhelming, especially if they have never performed a task of this type. However, with proper guidance, this kind of project can lead to a deeper understanding of principles that cannot be achieved as effectively by conventional lessons and inspire the students in ways not found in other types of lessons. An example of a rubric for grading projects is given in Appendix H.

# CHAPTER 7

# OK, Now All My Students Will Love Science and Math, Right?

**I HAVE USED** all of the recommended methods. All of my students will be fully invested in my course now, right?

Although you should see significant improvement, no system will handle all situations. It is the nature of the complex world we live in that we will always find new and unforeseen problems. There will always be that student or group of students who, despite your best efforts, does not respond as you would like. Teachers have beaten themselves up over that one student or group of students they just could not reach.

In math and science, maybe more than any other subjects, it is important that teachers be realistic and refrain from blaming themselves for all failures. This is counterproductive and takes time away from constructive efforts. Teachers who can honestly state they are doing their best within the constraints of the job and using every technique they know to ensure their students' success need to relax.

This does not suggest that teachers should give up on these students. An honest, unemotional self-evaluation of the methods a teacher is using can lead to incremental improvement with time. Keeping a journal with thoughts on the success of lessons, the employment of classroom management techniques, and new ideas for later classes is an excellent way to ensure improvement.

Let's look at some other ideas.

## Keep It as Relevant as Possible.

As was stated earlier, relevancy can be used to enhance on-task behavior by connecting students' experiences and interests to the material as much as possible. Teachers need to keep a focus on this relevancy as much as they can within the constraints of the classroom environment. The more a teacher knows about his or her students, the better this technique can be applied.

## Demonstrations: Make Some Magic!

Sometimes a demonstration and discussion can do more to elucidate a concept or principle than a laboratory investigation can. Demonstrations are stripped of mathematics and the details of the scientific method and lay the concept or principle simply before the students. In addition, learning can be accomplished with a single set of equipment. For concepts or principles that require expensive equipment, this allows the learning to take place within budget constraints. Teachers often find that students who are not science oriented respond to demonstrations better than labs.

A demonstration has another advantage that cannot be ignored: It creates a chance to make some magic. There are a variety of demonstrations that can be placed before students that tweak their preconceived notions of how things work. These demonstrations may include optical illusions created by optical arrangements of mirrors and lenses, Van de Graf generators that create a variety of static electricity effects, and a variety of mechanical demonstrations that will mystify and amaze. Figure 7.1 provides an excellent demonstration of optical properties. A lit candle (blue) placed at the focus of a parabolic mirror will cause another unlit candle (red) at the focus of a second parabolic mirror, arranged as shown in the figure, to suddenly ignite. This can occur with the mirrors at remarkable distances from each other and demonstrates why these types of mirrors are used for satellite communications.

For students who are difficult to reach, these demonstrations provide a bridge to learning motivated by curiosity and excitement. It is recommended that teachers collect a variety of demonstrations that can be used as introductions to units and assistance for clarifying difficult principles. Starting a unit by eliciting curiosity and excitement sets a tone that can carry throughout the learning process.

## The Joy of Projects

There is some disagreement among teachers on the importance of projects in the learning process. Many teachers feel that students tend to use artwork and cute multimedia to hide the fact that they really haven't learned anything about the concepts and principles. Often, students do this because the teacher doesn't monitor and critique the process incrementally as the students are performing the tasks of the project.

Projects are most successful when the teacher and students agree on the detailed goals that should be accomplished and how the results should be presented. In addition, group projects must be monitored to make sure every member of the group contributes and learns from the process. It is recommended that a clear rubric with scheduled updates be presented to the students upfront and that the learning objectives be clearly outlined in the initial assignment of the project.

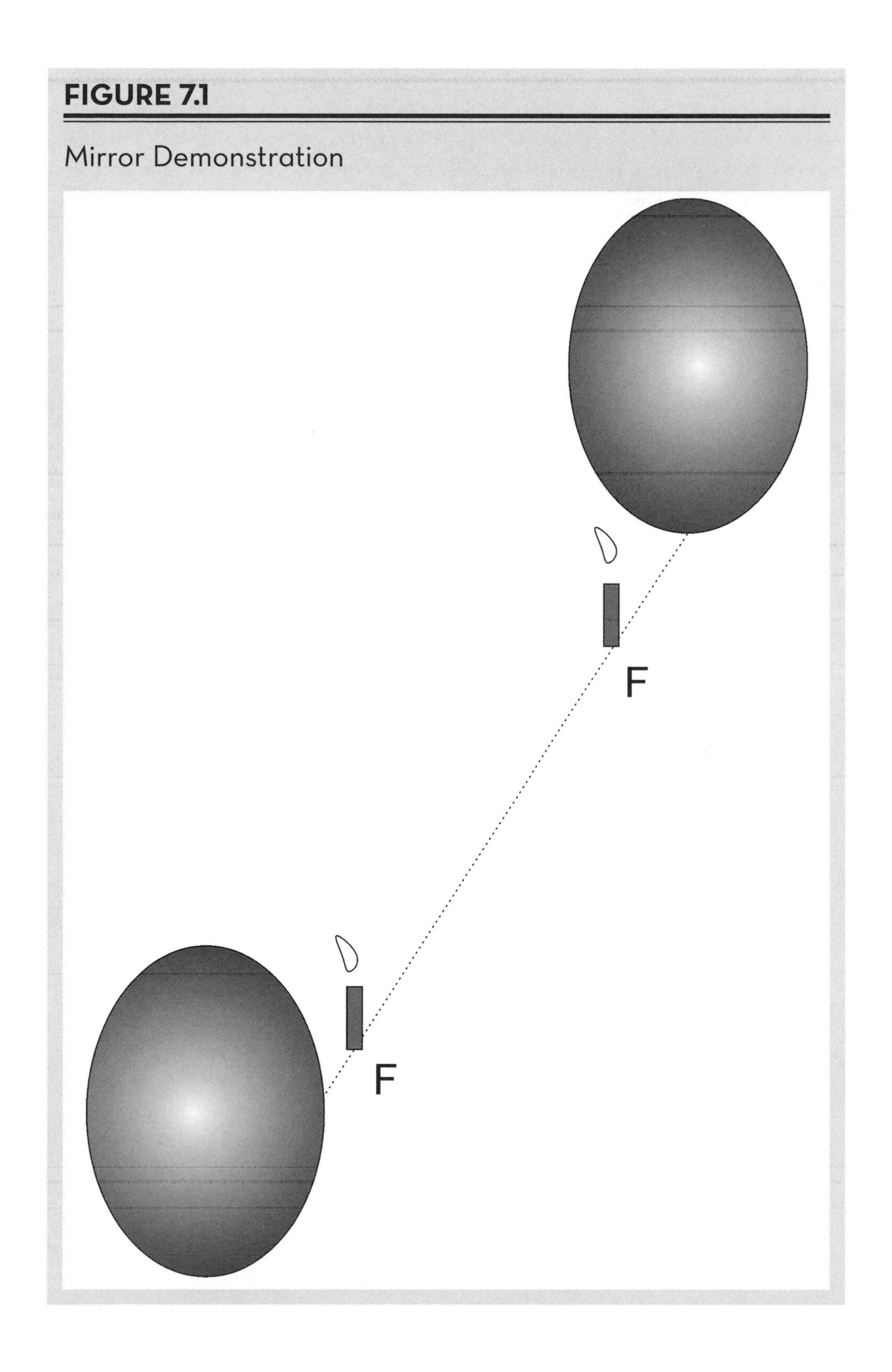


**FIGURE 7.1**

Mirror Demonstration

Although projects can be time-consuming and must be carefully monitored, they provide a real chance to connect learning to real-world events and issues. For the students who haven't thought about their future careers or need relevancy to remain focused on the subject, projects provide an avenue toward deeper understanding and enhanced appreciation of the material.

## Dealing With GT Students

All experienced teachers in upper-level classes have stories of that special student, one who challenged them and required a real effort to reach: the gifted and talented (GT) student.

These students are often bored with the standard curriculum and require a special effort by the teacher to meet their needs. These students are often as much a classroom management issue as a curriculum issue (Frasier and Passow 1994; Westberg and Archambault 1990–91). Boredom often leads these students to inappropriate behavior such as class disruption and challenges of the teacher during instruction. These students can be intimidating because they can be very blunt about their boredom and challenge the teacher intellectually, jumping on any perceived weaknesses in the teacher's presentation.

It is recommended that teachers have alternative instruction assignments ready for this kind of student. These assignments can include projects, advanced laboratory work, or reports on advanced topics. The internet is a good resource for these types of activities, as is the library. Another option is to urge these students to enter science project, engineering, and science team competitions.

Even with the special assignments, teachers must make sure students understand the standard curriculum in all areas. The special assignments and challenging material are used as an incentive to stay focused during the learning of the normal curriculum and allow the GT student to move ahead as other students take longer to work toward mastery.

## References

Frasier, M. M., and A. H. Passow. 1994. *Toward a new paradigm for identifying talent potential (Research Monograph 94112)*. Storrs, CT: National Research Center on the Gifted and Talented, University of Connecticut.

Westberg, K. L., and F. Archambault. 1990–91. *A study of successful classroom practices*. Storrs, CT: University of Connecticut.

# CHAPTER 8

# But I Still Don't Feel Comfortable Teaching This

**HEY, THAT IS** understandable. With the shortage of science and mathematics teachers, many teachers will be put in this position. Many teachers will find themselves teaching upper-level subjects they do not feel adequately prepared to teach. In smaller schools, there may even be an inadequate staff to provide support to these teachers. What specifically can these teachers expect?

- *Difficulty describing concepts and principles:* Discomfort with the material can often translate into inadequate descriptions during lessons.
- *Difficulty answering questions:* An immature understanding of the material can make it difficult for the teacher to answer student queries.
- *Challenges from the GT students:* Woe to the teacher who makes too many mistakes in front of these vultures! Oftentimes these students alleviate their boredom by flaying the unprepared teacher.
- *Difficulty formulating lessons:* A lack of understanding of a unit's material makes it much more difficult to formulate lessons and assessments.

So, now that you are really frightened, what can you do to mitigate your lack of knowledge and experience? Let's look at some strategies.

## The Importance of a Lesson Plan

A good lesson plan is crucial to a teacher's preparation to conduct a lesson. Teachers with good lesson plans tend to run a smoother and more efficient class and fumble less during the execution of the lesson. The form of a lesson plan can vary, but they all have certain basic parts (O'Bannon 2002):

- Heading
    - Teacher's name
    - Course name (and possibly the course number)
    - Lesson name
    - Necessary allotted time
    - Grade level
- Materials, media, and technology
    - Handouts, worksheets, presentations, photos, video, simulations, etc. (Do not include common classroom equipment.)
- Instructional objectives
    - General goals and long-range objectives
    - Lesson objectives, such as "The student will be able to (perform a skill, comprehend a concept or principle, remember facts, etc.)." These objectives need to be measurable, and the teacher should connect them to the students' prior knowledge.
- Instructional process
    - A set of steps defining the conduct of the lesson by the student and the teacher. Note that the lesson should be student-centered, relate to a student's real life, and have relevance to the students' prior knowledge. It is a good idea to number the steps.
        + Actions the teacher will take to teach the material
        + Actions the students will perform to reach the objectives

Note: In the eventuality that the lesson conforms to the 5E cycle or Modeling Instruction, these steps will conform to the steps of the cycle (5E) or the stages (Modeling Instruction).

- Closure
    - The student answers questions, explains concepts and principles, presents a product, and/or demonstrates skills pertaining to the objectives.

- Practice (conducted by the students)
    - Guided practice: Exercises and projects conducted in the classroom, with the teacher's guidance, to work toward achieving the objectives
    - Independent practice: Exercises and projects conducted at home to work toward achieving the objectives
- Assessments
    - Formative assessment or summative assessment over objectives
- Reflection and self-evaluation (performed after the lesson is conducted)
    - What in the lesson worked and what didn't
    - What should be done differently the next time the lesson is executed

Note that there is some disagreement about whether lesson plans should be written for each day or over an entire learning unit. The teacher should use what fits his or her teaching style. However, there are advantages to writing a unit lesson plan:

- A unit plan allows for some flexibility of schedule. It is sometimes difficult to gauge the time necessary to conduct a lesson. This can be especially difficult when applying the 5E cycle or Modeling Instruction. By setting the allotted time over a period of days, the teacher can adjust the daily timetable to account for unforeseen eventualities that may cause a daily lesson to be longer than anticipated.
- A unit lesson plan can allow the teacher to see the entire structure of the lesson. This can lead to clarity of purpose and better efficiency.

## Get Ahead and Stay Ahead.

The GT students in a class can be unkind to a teacher they perceive to be unprepared or less than knowledgeable. Once the students believe a teacher is not up to teaching the material, it is difficult to regain trust and respect.

An inexperienced teacher can protect against this abuse by working exercises and units well before they present them to the students, making the mistakes, alleviating deficiencies, and improving understanding in private. This also allows the teacher to consult with more experienced colleagues on particularly challenging units and problems.

## Take a Class.

Teachers have more options to take classes than ever before. Teachers who need additional training to improve their teaching can take courses at community or junior colleges, or take advantage of online offerings. It should also be noted that teachers may be able to use the materials from their coursework in their teaching (with instructor permission).

Ideally, teachers should begin these courses well before they start teaching the course to stay ahead of the curriculum. Summer courses are ideal for this purpose.

## Join Organizations.

Opportunities for networking and support can be found within organizations whose expressed purpose is to assist teachers in science and mathematics instruction. All teachers should join and participate in their local, state, and national associations' professional development opportunities.

The national organizations that support general education include the following:

- National Education Association (NEA)
- American Federation of Teachers (AFT)
- Association for Supervision and Curriculum Development (ASCD)

The national organizations that support science education and research include the following:

- General science education and research
  - National Science Teachers Association (NSTA)
  - Association of Science-Technology Centers (ASTC)
  - Society for Advancement of Chicanos and Native Americans in Science (SACNAS)
  - National Association for Research in Science Teaching (NARST)
  - Association for Science Teacher Education (ASTE)
  - School Science and Mathematics Association (SSMA)
  - The International Association for Science, Technology & Society (IASTS)
  - Science Service
  - National Academy of Sciences
  - American Association for the Advancement of Science (AAAS)
  - National Academy of Sciences (NAS)
  - National Science Foundation (NSF)
  - National Research Council (NRC)

- Chemistry education and research
    - American Chemical Society
- Physics education and research
    - American Association of Physics Teachers (AAPT)
    - Physics Teachers Education Coalition (PhysTEC)
    - American Physical Society (APS)

The national organizations that support mathematics education and research include the following:

- National Council of Teachers of Mathematics (NCTM)
- American Mathematical Society (AMS)
- American Statistical Association (ASA)
- Association for Women in Mathematics (AWM)
- Consortium for Mathematics and Its Applications (COMAP)
- Mathematical Association of America (MAA)

The websites for many of these organizations have forums where a teacher can join discussions with teachers who have similar interests and issues. Teachers can go to these forums to ask or answer questions, give or receive advice, and request or provide learning materials. These organizations also offer a variety of books, papers, and articles to keep teachers aware of the latest research and techniques in their field and in general education.

Attending local, state, regional, or national conferences held by these organizations is a great way for teachers to network with fellow science and mathematics teachers and find mentors. These conferences also provide an opportunity for teachers to keep up with the latest research and techniques in science and math education, as well as the latest discoveries in these subjects.

## Make Friends.

Even in cases where the support system in a school or school district is lacking, today's technology provides an unprecedented opportunity for teachers to find mentors and help with difficult concepts, problems, and issues. These include sites containing laboratory ideas, problems and solutions, and concept and principle descriptions beyond those in textbooks. Some sites contain simulations and virtual laboratories that can help increase comprehension.

A particularly good place to get help is the College Board website (*www.collegeboard.com*), which has discussion groups for different subjects. There are teachers who monitor the discussions and are more than willing to assist other teachers in need of help.

Finally, attending Advanced Placement Institutes and other conferences are a great way to get help in a variety of teaching areas and form lasting relationships with colleagues for the exchange of ideas and assistance.

## Expand Your Tool Set.

There are many tools and techniques available to new teachers beyond those presented in this book. New teachers, when they feel ready to expand their arsenals, will find a variety of new tools. These may be obtained from books, the internet, and fellow teachers.

One particularly good resource is the book *Teach Like a Champion* by Doug Lemov (Lemov 2010), which gives a variety of tools and techniques that can be used in the classroom. One particularly helpful aspect of this book is that it comes with a DVD that demonstrates these techniques in a real classroom so the teacher can see how each technique is incorporated. This is particularly useful because it often can be difficult for a working teacher to schedule time to observe other teachers in their classrooms.

## References

Lemov, D. 2010. *Teach like a champion: 49 techniques that put students on the path to college.* San Francisco, CA: Jossey-Bass.

O'Bannon, B. 2002. What is a lesson plan? Office of Information Technology, University of Tennessee, Knoxville. *http://itc.utk.edu/~bobannon/lesson_plan.html.*

# CHAPTER 9
## You Are Important!

**ALL TEACHERS HAVE** times when they don't feel as if they are really making a difference. In the best of circumstances, teaching is an extremely challenging and taxing profession. Teachers often feel overburdened, unsupported, and unappreciated with the constraints and regulations that define their world pressing down on them as they try to do their jobs. Many teachers find they cannot handle the environment. The low national retention rate among young teachers (those who have less than six years of teaching experience) is a testament to the frustration that can occur.

The problem is even more pronounced with mathematics and science teachers, as demonstrated by even lower retention rates. These teachers, frustrated and burned out, often leave their teaching positions to take higher-paying positions with lower stress outside education.

So how does a young teacher stay positive and focused in such an environment? Even with all the assistance provided in this book, teaching is and will remain a challenging profession. Surviving in education is a matter of teachers setting realistic goals and expectations and seeing the big picture of the value of their work. Teachers need to set incremental and achievable goals of improvement that they can work toward each year—goals based on self-reflection during the school year. It is important that the teacher understand that with reflection and goal setting, he or she can make progress toward teaching mastery over time with adequate patience, perseverance, and a positive attitude.

In addition, teachers need to see that what they do contributes to a greater good and remind themselves of the importance of their product: educated young people who will be the foundation for future progress. That somewhat troublesome student in your class often can become a wonderful adult as he matures and grows academically. It can be difficult to believe this when Johnny is sitting in your class staring at the ceiling during group work, but he may be a future business or community leader who just hasn't found his niche yet.

One fact is unassailable: There is no more important or noble profession than teaching. Teachers serve a vital role in defining the health of a future society. It is not uncommon for a teacher to send a student to college who is the first student in his family to attend, or maybe a student who lives in a socioeconomically deprived community gets an advanced education and comes back to help solve problems in her neighborhood. These are the opportunities and rewards that must motivate teachers to stay strong, progress toward instructional mastery, and work toward student success.

# APPENDIX A

## Naive Conceptions in Physics

| Topic | Conceptions |
|---|---|
| Overall/kinematics | • History has no place in science.<br>• Two objects side by side must have the same speed.<br>• Acceleration and velocity are always in the same direction.<br>• Velocity is a force.<br>• If velocity is zero, then acceleration must be zero, too. |
| Falling bodies | • Heavier objects fall faster than lighter ones.<br>• Acceleration is the same as velocity.<br>• The acceleration of a falling object depends on its mass.<br>• Freely falling bodies can only move downward.<br>• There is no gravity in a vacuum.<br>• Gravity only acts on objects when they are falling. |
| Inertia | • Forces are required for motion with constant velocity.<br>• Inertia deals with the state of motion (at rest or in motion).<br>• All objects can be moved with equal ease in the absence of gravity.<br>• All objects eventually stop moving when the force is removed.<br>• Inertia is the force that keeps objects in motion.<br>• If two objects are both at rest, they have the same amount of inertia.<br>• Velocity is absolute and not dependent on the frame of reference. |
| Newton's laws | • Action-reaction forces act on the same body.<br>• There is no connection between Newton's laws and kinematics.<br>• The product of mass and acceleration, *ma*, is a force.<br>• Fiction can't act in the direction of motion.<br>• The normal force on an object is equal to the weight of the object by the 3rd law.<br>• The normal force on an object always equals the weight of the object.<br>• Equilibrium means that all the forces on an object are equal.<br>• Equilibrium is a consequence of the third law.<br>• Only animate things (people, animals) exert forces; passive ones (tables, floors) do not exert forces.<br>• Once an object is moving, heavier objects push more than lighter ones.<br>• Newton's third law can be overcome by motion (such as by a jerking motion).<br>• A force applied by a hand, for instance, still acts on an object after the object leaves the hand. |

| Topic | Conceptions |
|---|---|
| Gravitation | • The Moon is not falling.<br>• The Moon is not in free fall.<br>• The force that acts on an apple is not the same as the force that acts on the Moon.<br>• The gravitational force is the same on all falling bodies.<br>• There are no gravitational forces in space.<br>• The gravitational force acting on the space shuttle is nearly zero.<br>• The gravitational force acts on one mass at a time.<br>• The Moon stays in orbit because the gravitational force on it is balanced by the centrifugal force acting on it.<br>• Weightlessness means there is no gravity.<br>• The Earth's spinning motion causes gravity. |
| Conservation of energy | • Energy gets used up or runs out.<br>• Something that is not moving can't have any energy.<br>• A force acting on an object does work even if the object does not move.<br>• Energy is destroyed in transformations from one type to another.<br>• Energy can be recycled.<br>• Gravitational potential energy is the only type of potential energy.<br>• When an object is released to fall, the gravitational potential energy immediately becomes all kinetic energy.<br>• Energy is not related to Newton's laws.<br>• Energy is a force. |
| Conservation of momentum | • Momentum is not a vector.<br>• Conservation of momentum applies only to collisions.<br>• Momentum is the same as force.<br>• Moving masses in the absence of gravity do not have momentum.<br>• The center of mass of an object must be inside the object.<br>• Center of mass is always the same as the center of gravity.<br>• Momentum is not conserved in collisions with "immovable" objects.<br>• Momentum and kinetic energy are the same. |
| Circular motion | • Circular motion does not require a force.<br>• Centrifugal forces are real.<br>• An object moving in a circle with constant speed has no acceleration.<br>• An object moving in a circle will continue in circular motion when released.<br>• An object in circular motion will fly out radially when released. |
| Torque and angular momentum | • Any force acting on an object will produce a torque.<br>• Objects moving in a straight line cannot have angular momentum.<br>• Torque is the same as force and is in the same direction.<br>• Angular momentum is not a vector.<br>• The direction of angular momentum is in the direction of linear momentum. |

| Topic | Conceptions |
|---|---|
| Kepler's laws | • Planetary orbits are circles.<br>• The speed of a planet in orbit never changes.<br>• An object must be at both foci of an elliptical orbit.<br>• All the planets move in their orbits with the same speed.<br>• No work is done on orbiting planets by the Sun.<br>• The orbits of the planets lie precisely in the same plane.<br>• All the planets revolve about the Sun with the same period.<br>• Revolution is the same as rotation. |
| Navigating in space | • Spacecraft travel in straight lines from one planet to another.<br>• Spacecraft can be launched anytime to travel from one planet to another.<br>• Spacecraft are not affected by the Sun.<br>• Motion relative to Earth is the same as motion relative to the Sun.<br>• Jets can fly in space.<br>• Spacecraft in orbit about Earth don't follow a sinusoidal path relative to the Sun.<br>• Rockets need something (air) to push against. |
| Curved space and black holes | • Space is not something.<br>• Black holes are big.<br>• Light always travels in straight lines.<br>• Black holes exert a greater gravitational force on distant objects than the star from which they were formed.<br>• Observations made in a gravitational field are different than those made in a system undergoing constant acceleration.<br>• Things in space make sounds.<br>• If the Sun were to become a black hole, the Earth would get sucked into it. |
| Temperature and gas laws | • A cold body contains no heat.<br>• There is no limit on the lowest temperature.<br>• At absolute zero, motion of every part of an object stops.<br>• An object has no mass at absolute zero.<br>• Sweaters will make you warmer.<br>• Cold can flow.<br>• Gases can be compressed to zero volume.<br>• Heat and temperature are the same thing.<br>• Heat and cold flow like liquids.<br>• Pressure is the same as force.<br>• Skin is a good thermometer. |
| Harmonic motion | • The period of oscillation depends on amplitude.<br>• The restoring force is constant at all points in the oscillation.<br>• The heavier a pendulum bob, the shorter its period.<br>• All pendulum motion is perfect simple harmonic motion for any initial angle.<br>• Harmonic oscillators go forever.<br>• A pendulum accelerates through the lowest point of its swing.<br>• Amplitude of oscillations is measured peak to peak.<br>• The acceleration is zero at the end points of the motion of a pendulum. |

# APPENDIX A

| Topic | Conceptions |
|---|---|
| Introduction to waves | • Waves transport matter.<br>• There must be a medium through which a wave can travel.<br>• Waves do not have energy.<br>• All waves travel the same way.<br>• Frequency is connected to loudness for all amplitudes.<br>• Big waves travel faster than small waves in the same medium.<br>• Different colors of light are different types of waves.<br>• Pitch is related to intensity. |
| Wave nature of light | • Light just exists and has no origin.<br>• Light is a particle.<br>• Light is a mixture of particles and waves.<br>• Light waves and radio waves are not the same thing.<br>• In refraction, the characteristics of light change.<br>• The speed of light never changes.<br>• Rays and wave fronts are the same thing.<br>• There is no interaction between light and matter.<br>• The addition of all colors of light yields black.<br>• Double slit interference shows light wave crests and troughs.<br>• Light exists in the crest of a wave and dark in the trough.<br>• In refraction, the frequency (color) of light changes.<br>• Refraction is the bending of waves. |
| Michelson-Morley experiment | • A null result means the experiment was a failure.<br>• The ether exists because something must transmit light.<br>• Relativistic effect (length contraction) is the reason why no difference in the speed of light was observed. |
| Special relativity | • Velocities for light are additive as for particles.<br>• Postulates cannot be used to develop a theory.<br>• Length, mass, and time changes are just apparent.<br>• Time is absolute.<br>• Length and time only change for one observer.<br>• Time dilation refers to two clocks in two different frames.<br>• Time dilation and length contractions have not been proven in experiments.<br>• There exists a preferred frame of reference in the universe.<br>• A mass moving at the speed of light becomes energy.<br>• Mass is absolute—that is, it has the same value in all reference frames. |

| Topic | Conceptions |
|---|---|
| Fundamental forces | • All forces have to be contact forces.<br>• The gravitational force is the only natural force.<br>• All forces are unique, so none are fundamental.<br>• The gravitational force is the strongest force.<br>• The gravitational and electromagnetic forces are more fundamental than the strong and weak nuclear forces.<br>• Electricity and magnetism are two different forces.<br>• The weak and strong nuclear forces are really the same force.<br>• All forces are equally effective over all ranges.<br>• None of the fundamental forces have been proven to exist.<br>• The electrical force is the same as the gravitational force. |
| Electric fields and forces | • A moving charge will always follow a field line as it accelerates.<br>• If a charge is not on a field line, it feels no force.<br>• Field lines are real.<br>• Coulomb's law applies to charge systems that consist of something other than point charges.<br>• A charged body has only one type of charge.<br>• The electric field and force are the same thing and in the same direction.<br>• Field lines can begin and end anywhere.<br>• There are a finite number of field lines.<br>• Fields don't exist unless there is something to detect them.<br>• Forces at a point exist without a charge there.<br>• Field lines are paths of a charges motion.<br>• The electric force is the same as the gravitational force.<br>• Field lines actually radiate from positive to negative charges and convey motion.<br>• Field lines exist only in two dimensions. |
| Millikan experiment | • Charge is continuous and can occur in any amount.<br>• An electron is pure negative charge with no mass.<br>• Oil drops are electrons.<br>• The scientific method is pure and absolute.<br>• Scientists always stumble on discoveries.<br>• Millikan measured the mass of the electron. |
| Equipotentials and fields | • Voltage flows through a circuit.<br>• There is no connection between voltage and electric field.<br>• Voltage is energy.<br>• Equipotential means equal field or uniform field.<br>• High voltage by itself is dangerous.<br>• It takes work to move a real charge on an equipotential.<br>• Charges move by themselves.<br>• Sparks occur when an electric field pulls charges apart. |

| Topic | Conceptions |
|---|---|
| Potential difference and capacitance | • A capacitor and a battery operate on the same principle.<br>• A potential difference is only on plates of a capacitor and not in the region between them.<br>• Charge flows through a dielectric such as glass.<br>• Designations of (+) and (-) are absolute.<br>• $Q = CV$ is a basic conceptual law.<br>• No work is required to charge a capacitor.<br>• A capacitor requires two separate pieces.<br>• There is a net charge on a capacitor.<br>• The capacitance of a capacitor depends on the amount of charge.<br>• A positive charged capacitor plate only has positive charges on it.<br>• Charges flow through a capacitor. |
| Simple DC circuits | • Resistors consume charge.<br>• Electrons move quickly (near the speed of light) through a circuit.<br>• Charges slow down as they go through a resistor.<br>• Current is the same thing as voltage.<br>• There is no current between the terminals of a battery.<br>• The bigger the container, the larger the resistance.<br>• A circuit does not have to form a closed loop for a current to flow.<br>• Current gets "used up" as it flows through a circuit.<br>• A conductor has no resistance.<br>• The resistance of a parallel combination is larger than the largest resistance.<br>• Current is an excess charge.<br>• Charges that flow in a circuit are from the battery.<br>• The bigger the battery, the more voltage it has.<br>• Power and energy are the same thing.<br>• Batteries create energy out of nothing. |
| Magnetic fields | • North and south magnetic poles are the same as positive and negative charges.<br>• Magnetic field lines start at one pole and end at the other.<br>• Poles can be isolated.<br>• Flux is the same as field lines.<br>• Flux is actually the flow of the magnetic field.<br>• Magnetic fields are the same as electric fields.<br>• Charges at rest can experience magnetic forces.<br>• Magnetic fields from magnets are not caused by moving charges.<br>• Magnetic fields are not three-dimensional.<br>• Magnetic field lines hold you on Earth.<br>• Charges, when released, will move toward the poles of a magnet. |

| Topic | Conceptions |
|---|---|
| Electromagnetic induction | • Generating electricity requires no work.<br>• When generating electricity, only the magnet can move.<br>• Voltage can only be induced in a closed circuit.<br>• Magnetic flux, rather than change of magnetic flux, causes an induced EMF.<br>• All electric fields must start on (+) and end on (−) charges.<br>• Water in dams causes electricity. |
| Alternating current | • Charges move all the way around a circuit and all the way back.<br>• Voltage and current remain constant, as in DC circuits.<br>• Energy is not lost in a transformer.<br>• A step-up transformer gives you something more for less input.<br>• Transformers can be used to change DC voltages.<br>• Electrical companies supply the electrons for your household current. |
| Wave-particle duality | • Light is one or the other—a particle or a wave—only.<br>• Light can be a particle at one point in time and a wave at another point in time.<br>• Particles can't have wave properties.<br>• Waves can't have particle properties.<br>• The position of a particle always can be exactly known.<br>• A photon is a particle with a wave inside.<br>• Photons of higher frequency are bigger than photons of lower frequency.<br>• All photons have the same energy.<br>• Intensity means that the amplitude of a photon is bigger.<br>• The uncertainty principle results from the limits of measuring devices.<br>• Laser beams are always visible by themselves.<br>• Sometimes you feel like a wave, sometimes you don't. |
| Models of the atom | • There is only one correct model of the atom.<br>• Electrons in an atom orbit nuclei like planets orbit the Sun.<br>• Electron clouds are pictures of orbits.<br>• Electrons can be in any orbit they wish.<br>• Hydrogen is a typical atom.<br>• The wave function describes the trajectory of an electron.<br>• Electrons are physically larger than protons.<br>• Electrons and protons are the only fundamental particles.<br>• Physicists currently have the "right" model of the atom.<br>• Atoms can disappear (decay). |

Note: This table is adapted from the work of Dr. Richard Olenick at the University of Dallas, *http://phys.udallas.edu/C3P/Preconceptions.pdf*

# APPENDIX B

## Interactive Notebook Rubric

- Right-hand pages
  - Note pages have titles and page numbers. (5%)
  - Notes are complete and readable. (25%)
  - Notes are in Cornell notes form. (10%)
- Left-hand pages
  - Student work pages have titles and page numbers. (5%)
  - Student work is complete and follows instructions. (25%)
  - Student work is neat and readable. (10%)
  - Provide a 10% bonus for creativity (e.g., art, photos, foldables, multimedia).
- Table of contents
  - Table of contents exists. (10%)
  - Table of contents has a title, proper labels, and page numbers. (10%)

# APPENDIX C
## Equation Map Rubric

- Equation is written in standard form. (20%)
- Complete word definitions are given for each variable with units. (20% for the definitions; 10% for the units given correctly; 10% for the association lines)
- The equation is solved for every possible variable, with a word description of the application. (20% for the algebra; 20% for the word descriptions)

BONUS: State limitations of applicability of the equation. (5%)

# APPENDIX D

## Key Terms and Key Problems for Physics Principles

| Physics Principles | Keys |
|---|---|
| One-dimensional kinematics | **Terms:** distance, displacement, time, velocity, speed, acceleration, deceleration, braking, height, constant acceleration, constant braking, free fall, initial conditions, kinematic equations<br><br>**Problems:** constant acceleration and deceleration of the horizontal motion of objects; objects falling straight down in vacuum; objects thrown straight up in vacuum; motion on an inclined plane |
| Two-dimensional kinematics | **Terms:** projectile, trajectory, path, range, height, apex, initial conditions, kinematic equations<br><br>**Problems:** projectile motion with no friction; streaming water from a hose, hole, or leak |
| Newton's first law of motion | **Terms:** forces (gravitational, normal, friction, tension, buoyancy, electric, magnetic), free-body diagram, total force, net force, Newton's first law of motion, Newton's third law of motion<br><br>**Problems:** any motion with object at rest or moving with constant velocity |
| Newton's second law of motion | **Terms:** forces (gravitational, normal, friction, tension, buoyancy, electric, magnetic), free-body diagram, total force, net force, mass, acceleration, Newton's second law of motion, Newton's third law of motion<br><br>**Problems:** any motion with object moving with constant acceleration |

| Physics Principles | Keys |
|---|---|
| Circular motion and universal gravitation; Kepler's laws | **Terms:** circular motion, centripetal, centrifugal, radial, pseudoforce, radius, Newton's second law for circular motion, apparent weight, universal gravitation, universal gravitation law, orbit (circular, elliptical, hyperbolic), Kepler's laws, area subtended, time (orbiting object), average radius, period<br><br>**Problems:** any force or force combination causing uniform circular motion; any motion with the acceleration perpendicular to the velocity; calculation of gravity force between two masses with a given distance between their centers; circular orbit problems; elliptical orbit period and average radius comparisons; motion in a magnetic field |
| Work and power | **Terms:** force, displacement, time, conservative force, nonconservative force, energy dissipated, work, power, friction<br><br>**Problems:** applying a force to an object that moves the object over some displacement; simple machine problems (incline or ramp, screw, lever, pulley, wedge, block and tackle, wheel and axle); complex machine problems |
| Conservation of energy | **Terms:** conservation of energy, kinetic energy, potential energy (gravitational or spring), heat, work, mass, speed and velocity, height, acceleration due to gravity, spring constant, compression, stretch, closed system, work<br><br>**Problems:** falling objects in vacuum; roller-coaster problems with no friction; pendulum problems; elastic collisions; general orbital motion |
| Work-energy principle | **Terms:** work-energy principle, net (total) work, change in kinetic energy, mass, velocity<br><br>**Problems:** problems involving objects that change velocity due to work on them but whose motion does not change the potential energy, usually horizontal motion |
| Generalized work-energy principle | **Terms:** generalized work-energy principle, kinetic energy, potential energy (gravitational or spring), heat, work, mass, speed/velocity, height, acceleration due to gravity, spring constant, compression, stretch, closed system, work, nonconservative work/force, friction<br><br>**Problems:** falling objects with air friction; roller-coaster problems with friction; pendulum problems with friction |

| Physics Principles | Keys |
|---|---|
| Generalized Newton's second law | **Terms:** generalized Newton's second law, external force, rate of change of momentum<br><br>**Problems:** motion of object with changing mass (rockets, leaking object) |
| Momentum conservation | **Terms:** momentum conservation, momentum, mass, velocity, collision, impact, explosion, decay, merge and combine, elastic, inelastic<br><br>**Problems:** collision problems (elastic and inelastic); explosion and decay problems |
| Impulse | **Terms:** impulse, impact, bounce, brake, accelerate, average force, time, change in momentum<br><br>**Problems:** impact problems with an average impact force; problems with nonconstant braking or nonconstant acceleration; bounce problems |
| Rotational kinematics | **Terms:** extended bodies, rotation, axes, angular displacement, angular velocity, angular acceleration, time<br><br>**Problems:** calculations of angular displacement, angular velocity, angular acceleration, and time for rotating extended bodies |
| Rotational Newton's laws | **Terms:** rotational Newton's laws, extended bodies, rotation, axes, torque (moment), angular velocity, moment of inertia, angular acceleration<br><br>**Problems:** Calculations involving torques on an extended body that is not rotating or is rotating with constant angular velocity (see-saw balancing, signs hung on extended bodies); calculations involving torques on an extended body and its relationship to the moment of inertia and angular acceleration of the extended body (turning a door knob or handle, turning a wrench, motors and generators) |
| Statics | **Terms:** statics, extended bodies, rotation, axes, torque (moment), force<br><br>**Problems:** problems with extended bodies where they are not translating or rotating (ladder stability problems; architectural structures) |

# APPENDIX D

| Physics Principles | Keys |
| --- | --- |
| Dynamics | **Terms:** dynamics, extended bodies, rotation, axes, torque (moment), angular velocity, moment of inertia, angular acceleration, right-hand rule, force, mass, acceleration<br><br>**Problems:** problems with angular acceleration and/or linear acceleration of extended bodies (problems with massive pulleys and wheels, cables, ropes, strings, chains, and accelerating masses) |
| Rotational work | **Terms:** rotational work, torque (moment), angular displacement, right-hand rule<br><br>**Problems:** calculation of work to rotate an extended body by a torque through a given angular displacement |
| Conservation of energy with rotation | **Terms:** conservation of energy with rotation, extended bodies, rotation, axes, rotational kinetic energy, general kinetic energy, right-hand rule<br><br>**Problems:** rolling massive extended bodies on a random hill course; vehicles with massive wheels |
| Rotational work-energy principle | **Terms:** extended bodies, rotation, axes, rotational kinetic energy, general kinetic energy, net (total) work, right-hand rule<br><br>**Problems:** rolling massive extended bodies on a horizontal where the net work causes a change in the general kinetic energy |
| Generalized rotational work-energy principle | **Terms:** generalized rotational work-energy principle, extended bodies, rotation, axes, rotational kinetic energy, general kinetic energy, nonconservative work, friction, right-hand rule<br><br>**Problems:** rolling massive extended bodies on a random hill course with friction; vehicles with massive wheels and friction |
| Generalized rotational Newton's second law | **Terms:** generalized rotational Newton's second law, extended bodies, rotation, axes, torque (moment), change in angular momentum, precession, nutation, right-hand rule<br><br>**Problems:** problems with gyroscopes and precession; bicycle wheels turning |

| **Physics Principles** | **Keys** |
|---|---|
| Conservation of angular momentum | **Terms:** conservation of angular momentum, extended bodies, rotation, axes, torque (moment), angular momentum, precession, nutation, right-hand rule, center of gravity and mass, roll, pitch, yaw<br><br>**Problems:** problems concerning the calculation of rotational motion for extended objects with changing moment of inertia (spinning skater or dancer, dropped object on a spinning turntable, bicycle stability) |
| Equilibrium, stability, and elasticity | **Terms:** first condition of equilibrium, second condition of equilibrium, stable equilibrium (dynamic stability, dynamic instability), unstable equilibrium, neutral equilibrium, elasticity, elastic region, proportional limit, elastic limit, plastic region, breaking point, fracture, stress, strain, elongation and compression, elastic and Young's modulus, shear, shear modulus, bulk, bulk modulus<br><br>**Problems:** calculation of equilibrium; calculation of deformations (elongation and compression, shear, bulk) for a given stress; calculation of moduli (elastic and Young's, shear, bulk) from stress and strain |
| Archimedes' principle | **Terms:** Archimedes' principle, buoyancy, float, displacement of liquid and air, submerge, density, volume, mass<br><br>**Problems:** buoyancy problems; flotation problems; density acquisition by displacement of liquids problems |
| Pascal's principle | **Terms:** pressure, gauge pressure, density, acceleration due to gravity, height, motionless fluids, incompressible<br><br>**Problems:** calculation of pressure at a given depth in a body of liquid with no flow |
| Bernoulli's principle | **Terms:** Bernoulli's principle, density, height, velocity, pressure, gauge pressure<br><br>**Problems:** calculation of incompressible fluid flows with no or little viscosity (pipes, hoses, leaking buckets, fountains, faucets and spigots, water pumps, water towers) |
| Continuity equation | **Terms:** continuity equation, constriction, expand, hose and pipe dimensions (area, radius, diameter), velocity, density<br><br>**Problems:** hose, pipe, and vent flow problems with varying hose, pipe, and vent dimensions (radius, dimension, and area) |

| Physics Principles | Keys |
|---|---|
| Thermal effects on matter | **Terms:** heat, specific heat, specific heat equation, mass, temperature, thermal equilibrium, phase change (melting and freezing, boiling and condensation, sublimation and deposition, evaporation), heat and enthalpy of vaporization and condensation, heat and enthalpy of fusion and melting, heat and enthalpy of sublimation and deposition, triple point, triple point diagram, thermal expansion<br><br>**Problems:** heat and temperature change (specific heat) problems (with and without phase change); thermal equilibrium problems (with and without phase changes); thermal expansion problems |
| Heat transfer | **Terms and problems:** conduction (solids, bars, rods, plates and panels, insulation), convection (heating and cooling systems, heating water in a pan, water cycle), radiation (sun, fire, radiator) |
| Gas laws | **Terms:** ideal gas law, Boyle's law, Charles' law, Gay-Lussac law, combined gas law, pressure, volume, temperature, moles, universal gas constant, density, molecule speeds<br><br>**Problems:** all gas law problems relating volume, pressure, temperature, and moles at typical conditions; all gas law problems for processes where volume, pressure, or temperature is changed and how that change affects the others |
| Thermal processes; first and second laws of thermodynamics | **Terms:** first law of thermodynamics, second law of thermodynamics, pressure, volume, temperature, work, heat, internal energy, ideal gas, P-V diagram, isobaric process, isochoric process, isothermal process, adiabatic process, cyclic process, Carnot cycle, efficiency, entropy, disorder<br><br>**Problems:** calculation of internal energy change, work, heat, and efficiency for various thermodynamic processes on a P-V diagram; calculation of entropy change for systems and their surroundings (and process spontaneity) for various thermodynamic processes |
| Basic wave properties | **Terms:** frequency, period, wavelength, amplitude, phase, spatial, temporal, node, antinode, crest, trough, transverse, longitudinal, compression, sinusoidal and periodic waves, pulse wave, square wave, sawtooth wave, wave equation<br><br>**Problems:** calculation of frequency, wavelength, or wave velocity using $f\lambda = v$; calculations involving solution of wave travel distance, wave velocity, or wave travel time using $d = vt$; calculation of frequency from the period; calculation of period from the frequency; calculation of frequency using $f$ = number of waves/time |

| Physics Principles | Keys |
|---|---|
| Basic wave behaviors | **Terms:** reflection, refraction, diffraction, interference, superposition, constructive interference, destructive interference, fixed boundary conditions, free boundary conditions, standing wave, resonance, Doppler effect<br><br>**Problems:** reflection of longitudinal waves from boundaries; reflection of transverse waves from free and fixed boundaries; changing of wave properties when refracting; superposition of two or more waves at the same location; Doppler calculations |
| Sound and music | **Terms:** all terms for basic wave properties and basic wave behaviors + loudness, decibels, intensity, fundamental, harmonic(s), note, pitch, spectrum, timbre, consonance, musical interval, chord, octave, dissonance, beat, noise, diffraction<br><br>**Problems:** calculation of resonator geometry (string length, open pipe length, closed pipe length, bar length) from frequency and wavelength of fundamental/harmonic(s); calculation of frequency and wavelength of fundamental/harmonic(s) from resonator geometry (string length, open pipe length, closed pipe length, bar length); calculation of frequency and wavelength ratios for musical intervals; calculations on fixed strings (both ends) involving frequencies and wavelengths of fundamental and harmonic(s), length, tension, and density; calculation of beats given the pitch of two notes; Doppler calculations with sound; calculation of interference of multiple sound sources |
| Light and electromagnetic waves | **Terms:** all terms for basic wave properties and basic wave behaviors + speed of light, luminous flux, luminous intensity, luminous energy, luminance, illuminance, luminous emittance, color (primary, complimentary, RGB), color mixing (dyes, light), reflection law, Snell's law, angle of incidence, angle of reflection, angle of refraction, index of refraction, total internal reflection, polarization (linear, circular, elliptical) lasers, interference patterns (single slit, multiple slits, diffraction grating, interferometer, thin films), diffraction<br><br>**Problems:** calculation of frequency and wavelength for light using $f\lambda = c$; calculation of luminous flux, luminous intensity, luminous energy, luminance, illuminance, and/or luminous emittance given source or reflector geometry; color mixing; calculation of reflection geometry; calculation of refraction geometry; calculation of total internal reflection geometry; calculation of polarization angles and amplitudes; calculations involving interfering light from single slits, multiple slits, diffraction gratings, interferometers, and/or thin films; Doppler calculations with light |

| Physics Principles | Keys |
|---|---|
| Optics | **Terms:** lens-mirror formula, mirror (flat, concave, convex, spherical, parabolic, convergent, divergent), lens (double convex, double concave, convergent, divergent), source, focus, focal length, center of curvature, radius of curvature, image (real, virtual, erect, inverted, magnified, reduced), object distance, image distance, object height, image height, magnification, ray (real, virtual), ray tracing, compound optics, microscope, binoculars, telescope, periscope, spherical aberration, chromatic aberration<br><br>**Problems:** calculation of image distance, object distance, focal length, center of curvature, image height, object height, or magnification for various simple mirrors, thin lenses, and compound optics using the lens-mirror formula and ray tracing |
| Electrostatics (charges, electric field, and electric force) | **Terms:** charges (positive, negative), charging by induction, charging by conduction, electrostatic repulsion/attraction, electric force, electric field, electric field lines, poles, polarity, Coulomb's law, Gauss's law, charged plates, charged parallel plates, electroscope, pith balls<br><br>**Problems:** calculation of charge, force, electric field, and distance for various charge arrangements; electron motion in uniform electric fields |
| Electric potential and capacitors | **Terms:** electric potential formula (single charge), electric potential, electromotive force (EMF), voltage, equipotential lines, electric potential energy, battery/power supply, capacitor, capacitance, electron gun, charge<br><br>**Problems:** calculations involving charges in fields that do not move with constant acceleration (nonconstant electric fields) (electron guns, oil drop experiment) |
| DC circuits | **Terms:** electric components, electric conductor, electric insulator, current (direct [DC] and alternating [AC]), voltage, potential difference, potential gain, electromotive force (EMF), resistor, resistance, resistivity, capacitor, capacitance, switch, battery, power supply, voltmeter, ammeter, ohmmeter, Kirchoff's loop (voltage) law, Kirchoff's junction (current) law, Ohm's law, components in series, components in parallel, reducible circuits, irreducible circuits, RC circuit, short circuit<br><br>**Problems:** calculation of the current through a battery for a reducible circuit; calculation of resistance, current, and voltage for resistors in a reducible circuit; calculation of resistance, current, and voltage for resistors in an irreducible circuit; calculation of the resistance of a wire using resistivity; calculation of the voltage and current changes in an RC circuit |

| Physics Principles | Keys |
|---|---|
| AC circuits | **Terms:** alternating current, alternating current power supply, resistor, capacitor, inductor, mutual inductance, self inductance, transformers, reactance, impedance, Ohm's law, root-mean-square current/voltage (rms), maximum current/voltage, phase difference, RL circuit, RCL circuit, resonance circuit<br><br>**Problems:** calculation of reactance (capacitive, inductive) and impedance; calculation of rms and maximum values of the alternating currents and voltages; calculation of the frequency of a resonance circuit; transformer calculations |
| Magnetic fields and forces | **Terms:** moving charge(s), current(s), magnets, lodestones, magnetic poles, magnetic domains, ferromagnetism, magnetic field, Oersted law, Biot-Savart law, Ampere's law, magnetic field line, right-hand rule (curl type), magnetic force, Lorentz law, Laplace law, right-hand rule (cross product type), electromagnets, geomagnetism<br><br>**Problems:** calculation of magnetic field of a moving charge(s); calculation of magnetic field of a current carrying wire(s); calculation of magnetic field in the interior of a current-carrying coil and solenoid; tracing magnetic field lines with a compass; calculation of the force on a moving charge in a magnetic field (mass spectrometer); calculation of the force on a current carrying wire in a magnetic field (electric motors) |
| Magnetic induction | **Terms:** magnetic induction, magnetic flux, induced current and electromotive force, Faraday's law, Ohm's law, Lenz's law, right-hand rule (curl)<br><br>**Problems:** calculation of induced EMF/current for a changing magnetic flux (magnetic field changing and/or conducting loop area changing and/or angle of conducting loop changing relative to the field) (electric generators); calculation of EMF ratios for transformers; rail gun calculations; speakers and microphone operation |

| Physics Principles | Keys |
|---|---|
| Quantum mechanics/theory | **Terms:** quantum mechanics/theory, quantum property (quantum numbers for energy, angular momentum, spin), quantum state (wavefunction and probability distribution for particles), wave-particle duality, Planck radiation experiment, Compton scattering, photoelectric effect, Davisson-Germer experiment (DeBroglie hypothesis), Bohr spectra, Heisenberg uncertainty principle, quantum tunneling<br><br>**Problems:** photoelectric effect calculations; Compton effect calculations; Bohr spectra emission and absorption calculations; uncertainty calculations; Debroglie calculations |
| Atomic physics | **Terms:** Dalton's atomic model, plum pudding atomic model, Rutherford atomic model, Bohr atomic model, Schrodinger's atomic model, nucleus, proton, neutron, electron, energy levels, wavefunction, shells, suborbitals, orbitals, spins, photon, photon emmision and absorption, spectrum, spectral series, Fermions/Bosons<br><br>**Problems:** calculation of emitted and absorbed photon energies, frequencies, and wavelengths from energy level transitions; calculation of energy level differences from emitted and absorbed photon energy, wavelength, and frequency; determination of electron configurations for atoms; atomic bonding determination |
| Nuclear physics | **Terms:** neutron, proton, electron, positron, neutrino, antineutrino, alpha particle, alpha decay, beta decay, gamma decay, half-life, nuclear decay series, stability, mass number, atomic number, charge, fission, fusion, reactor, spontaneous decay, critical mass, chain reaction, mass-energy equivalence ($E = mc^2$)<br><br>**Problems:** calculation of half-life from timed amounts of nuclear material; nuclear reaction formula balancing; calculation of absorbed and released energy in nuclear reactions (mass deficit) |
| Special relativity | **Terms:** time dilation, length contraction, events, spontaneous events, light cone, frame transformations (Galilean, Lorentz), speed of light, Minkowski space, invariant quantity<br><br>**Problems (all assuming speeds at a significant fraction of the speed of light, no Galilean transformations):** frame transformation problems; velocity transformation problems; time dilation problems (twin paradox); length contraction problems; simultaneity problems; relativistic energy-momentum problems; calculation of invariant quantities |

# APPENDIX E

## Key Terms in Mathematics and Their Meanings

| Mathematics Operation | Key Words and Phrases | Selected Examples |
|---|---|---|
| Addition | increased by | The class increased by 15 students. |
| | more than | His collection had 10 cars more than before. |
| | combined | They combined their allowances to buy the present. |
| | together | Together they had 12 eggs. |
| | total, total of | There were 8 roses, 12 carnations, and 2 daisies. How many flowers did they have total? |
| | sum | The sum of their earnings was $28. |
| | added to | Her savings this week were added to her savings last week. |
| | altogether | How much money do they have altogether? |
| | both | Both of them have how much money? |
| | in all | How many carrots does she have in all? |
| | additional | If he had 10 additional baseball cards, how many would he have in all? |
| | all | If you combined all of their earnings, how much would they have? |
| | another | How many flowers would he have if you gave him another 3 more? |

| Mathematics Operation | Key Words and Phrases | Selected Examples |
|---|---|---|
| Subtraction | decreased by | The population of whales decreased by 400 in the past year. |
| | minus | She had $10, minus the amount she spent on the drink. How much did she have in all? |
| | less | She had 5 cards, less the 2 she gave to her brother. How many did she have in all? |
| | difference between/ difference of | What was the difference between their earnings last year? |
| | more than | Jacob has 6 more marbles than Carlos. |
| | less than | Carlos has 6 marbles less than Jacob. |
| | fewer than | Jenny has 6 fewer cookies than Elizabeth. |
| | how many more | How many more daisies does Kate have than Jacob? |
| | how much more | How much more money does Alex need to buy the computer? |
| | left | How many eggs are left? |
| | remain, remains | How many students remain on the bus? |
| | Words ending in "er"<br>Examples: higher, longer, heavier, larger, shorter, slower, farther | How much heavier is Jack's bag than Mark's?<br>How much farther does Susan need to run? |
| | take away | If Elizabeth takes away 2 of Jaime's baseball cards, how many will he have? |
| | only | Only 4 apples in the dozen were ripe. |

| Mathematics Operation | Key Words and Phrases | Selected Examples |
|---|---|---|
| Multiplication | of | Grandpa gave half of his share to Johnny. (multiplication by ½ ) |
| | times | John has 4 times as many jelly beans as Jake. |
| | multiplied by | The population multiplied by 12 over the past year. |
| | product of | The product of 4 and 7 |
| | increased by | The population of tigers in the wild increased by 10%. (multiplication by 0.10 and then addition) |
| | decreased by factor of | The population of rhinoceros living in the wild decreased by 25% in the past 10 years. (multiplication by 0.25 and then subtraction) |
| | every | Every apartment has 4 occupants. |
| | at this rate | Suzie makes 6 cupcakes per hour. At this rate, how many cupcakes will she make in 4 hours? |
| | in all | There are 12 rows with 6 plants in each row. How many plants are there in all? |
| | total | There are 8 rows with 7 plants in each row. How many plants are there total? |
| | each | Each pair of socks cost $1.50. How much will 6 pairs cost? |
| | doubled, tripled, quadrupled, etc. | The population of rabbits tripled in 2 years. |

# APPENDIX E

| Mathematics Operation | Key Words and Phrases | Selected Examples |
|---|---|---|
| Division | each | Pens cost $1 each. How many pens can you buy with $6? |
| | equal/equally | The items were packed equally into 3 bags. How many items were in each bag? |
| | per | The car gets 23 miles per gallon. How many gallons will it take to go 470 miles? |
| | separate | If the money was separated into equal shares, how much did each person get? |
| | a | Steak costs $3.69 a pound. How many pounds can you buy for $20? |
| | ratio *or* ratio of | If the student to teacher ratio was 27 to 1, how many teachers are there for 756 students? |
| | quotient *or* quotient of | The quotient of 20 and 4 is 5. |
| | Percent (division by 100) | What percentage of the population was over 18? |
| Equal | is | What is the sum of 8 and 4? |
| | are | What are the solutions of the equation $x^2-4 = 0$? |
| | was | What was the original number of apples on a cart if there are 12 left after 6 are removed? |
| | were | How many adult and child tickets were sold to a play if the cost of an adult ticket is $1.00, the price of a child ticket is $0.50, the total number of tickets sold is 100, and the revenue from sales totaled $75? |
| | will be | What will be the product if 6 is multiplied by 7? |
| | gives | Dividing 3 by 2 gives a quotient of 1.5. |
| | yields | Multiplying 4 by 7 yields a product of 28. |

Note: Table adapted from the work of Melissa Moreno, *www.gateways2learning.com*.

# APPENDIX F

## Problem-Solving Rubric

| Criteria | Achievement Level | | | |
|---|---|---|---|---|
| | **Achievement Level 1 (0%)** | **Achievement Level 2 (33%)** | **Achievement Level 3 (67%)** | **Achievement Level 4 (100%)** |
| Read the problem twice (5% weight) | 0%<br>No highlighting of numerical data and assumptions | 1% | 3% | 5%<br>Numerical data and assumptions are highlighted or underlined. |
| Connect concepts to principles (optional/ bonus) (0% weight) | 0%<br>Physical principles for the problem are not listed | 0% | 0% | 0%<br>Physical principles for the problem are listed. |
| Drawings or known and unknown lists (30% weight) | 0%<br>No drawing is given (assuming a drawing is possible) or no known or unknown variable list is given (assuming no drawing is possible). | 10%<br>Drawing is given (assuming a drawing is possible) or known or unknown variable list is given (assuming no drawing is possible), but the drawing or lists are missing parts or variables. | 20%<br>Drawing is given (assuming a drawing is possible) or known or unknown variable list is given (assuming no drawing is possible). The drawing or lists have all the parts, but the variables have improper names or are missing units. | 30%<br>Drawing is given (assuming a drawing is possible) or known or unknown variable list is given (assuming no drawing is possible). All parts are given, and all variables have proper names and units given. |

| Criteria | Achievement Level | | | |
|---|---|---|---|---|
| | Achievement Level 1 (0%) | Achievement Level 2 (33%) | Achievement Level 3 (67%) | Achievement Level 4 (100%) |
| Equation list (25% weight) | 0% No equations given | 8% Equations in the list are incorrect, incomplete, or not in correct order. | 16% Equations in the list are correct, given in correct order, and solved for the unknowns, but there are no check and question marks. | 25% Equations in the list are correct, given in correct order, and solved for the unknowns, and have check and question marks. |
| Substitute values and calculate (5% bonus for a correct answer) (20% weight) | 0% Values for knowns are not substituted on paper. | 7% Values for knowns are substituted on paper but with no units. | 14% Values for knowns are substituted with units but with no dimensional analysis performed. | 20% Values for knowns are substituted with units and with dimensional analysis performed. |
| Check the answer (20% weight) | 0% No check of the answer is performed. | 7% Answer checked with dimensional analysis only. | 14% Check of the answer beyond dimensional analysis is attempted but incorrect. | 20% Check of the answer beyond dimensional analysis is attempted and correct. |

# APPENDIX G

## Laboratory Report Rubric

| Criteria | Achievement Level | | | |
|---|---|---|---|---|
| | **Achievement Level 1 (0%)** | **Achievement Level 2 (33%)** | **Achievement Level 3 (67%)** | **Achievement Level 4 (100%)** |
| Title (4% Weight) | 0% Title is missing. | 1% Title is given but is not descriptive of the purpose of the laboratory investigation. | 2% Title is given but is only marginally descriptive of the purpose of the laboratory investigation. | 4% Title is given and is descriptive of the purpose of the laboratory investigation. |
| Background (6% Weight) | 0% Background is missing. | 2% Background is given but does not express the relevant prior knowledge (theory and data). | 4% Background is given but does not express the complete prior knowledge of the laboratory (theory and data). | 6% Background is given and represents complete prior knowledge (theory and data). |
| Purpose (10% Weight) | 0% Purpose is missing. | 3% Purpose is given but does not express the real purpose of the investigation. | 7% Purpose is given but does not give a complete purpose of the investigation. | 10% Purpose is given and clearly and completely expresses the purpose of the investigation. |

| Criteria | Achievement Level | | | |
|---|---|---|---|---|
| | Achievement Level 1 (0%) | Achievement Level 2 (33%) | Achievement Level 3 (67%) | Achievement Level 4 (100%) |
| Hypothesis (10% Weight) | 0% Hypothesis is missing. | 3% Hypothesis is given but does not reflect the purpose. | 7% Hypothesis is given and reflects the purpose, but is not an "if ... then" statement. | 10% Hypothesis is given, reflects the purpose, and is given as an "if ... then" statement. |
| Materials (10% Weight) | 0% Materials list is missing. | 4% Materials are given, but the list is incomplete. | 7% Materials are given and complete, but the item descriptions are vague or incomplete. | 10% Materials are given and complete, and the item descriptions are complete. |
| Procedure (15% Weight) | 0% Procedure is missing. | 5% Procedure is given but is not clear and descriptive of the actual process in the laboratory. | 10% Procedure is given and descriptive of the actual process in the laboratory, but not numbered and/or bulleted. | 15% Procedure is given, descriptive of the actual process in the laboratory, and numbered and/or bulleted. |
| Data analysis (15% Weight) | 0% Data analysis is missing. | 5% Data analysis is given but is missing parts that are specified in the procedure (tables, calculations, graphs). | 10% Data analysis is given with all parts that are specified in the procedure (tables, calculations, graphs), but these are not complete (i.e., significant figures). | 15% Data analysis is given with all parts that are specified in the procedure (tables, calculations, graphs), and these parts are complete. |
| Follow-up questions (15% Weight) | 0% Follow-up questions are missing. | 5% Follow-up questions are answered, but most are not answered correctly. Questions are not given with the answers. | 10% Follow-up questions are answered, and most are answered correctly. Questions are not given with the answers. | 15% Questions are answered, and most are answered correctly. Questions are given with the answers. |

| Criteria | Achievement Level | | | |
|---|---|---|---|---|
| | **Achievement Level 1 (0%)** | **Achievement Level 2 (33%)** | **Achievement Level 3 (67%)** | **Achievement Level 4 (100%)** |
| Conclusion (15% Weight) | 0%<br>Conclusion is missing. | 5%<br>Conclusion is given but does not have all three parts:<br>1. Is the hypothesis satisfied, and why?<br>2. State specific numbers and relationships found.<br>3. State all observed systematic errors, their effects on the results, and how they might be mitigated. | 10%<br>Conclusion is given and has all three parts:<br>1. Is the hypothesis satisfied, and why?<br>2. State specific numbers and relationships found.<br>3. State all observed systematic errors, their effects on the results, and how they might be mitigated.<br>Conclusion does not reflect the purpose and hypothesis. | 15%<br>Conclusion is given and has all three parts:<br>1. Is the hypothesis satisfied, and why?<br>2. State specific numbers and relationships found.<br>3. State all observed systematic errors, their effects on the results, and how they might be mitigated.<br>Conclusion reflects the purpose and hypothesis. |

# APPENDIX H

## Project Rubric

| Criteria | Achievement Level | | | |
|---|---|---|---|---|
| | **Achievement Level 1 (0%)** | **Achievement Level 2 (33%)** | **Achievement Level 3 (67%)** | **Achievement Level 4 (100%)** |
| Project purpose statement and initial plan (20% Weight) | 0% No purpose statement or initial plan is given. | 6% Either the purpose statement or the initial plan is missing. | 13% Purpose statement and initial plan are given, but are incomplete or vague. | 20% Purpose statement and initial plan are given and are complete and clear. |
| Review 1: Initial materials list and project plan (25% Weight) | 0% Student comes to review without the material list or project plan. | 8% Student comes to the review with either the materials list or the project plan missing. | 17% Student comes to the review with both the materials list and the project plan, but either or both are incomplete or vague. | 25% Student comes to the review with both the materials list and the project plan, and both are complete and clear. |
| Review 2: final materials list and project plan (25% Weight) | 0% Student comes to review without the material list or project plan. | 9% Student comes to the review with either the materials list or project plan missing. | 17% Student comes to the review with both the materials list and project plan, but either or both are incomplete or vague. | 25% Student comes to the review with both the materials list and the project plan, and both are complete and clear. |

| Criteria | Achievement Level | | | |
|---|---|---|---|---|
| | **Achievement Level 1 (0%)** | **Achievement Level 2 (33%)** | **Achievement Level 3 (67%)** | **Achievement Level 4 (100%)** |
| Final results (30% Weight) | 0% Student does not produce a final report, presentation, or device. | 10% Student produces a final report, presentation, and/or device, but it is incomplete or inoperable for demonstration. Report should include purpose statement, material list, final plan, results, and conclusion. | 20% Student produces a final report, presentation, and/or device, and it is complete or operable for demonstration. Report should include purpose statement, material list, final plan, results, and conclusion. Student is unable to make a presentation and/or answer questions pertaining to the project. | 30% Student produces a final report, presentation, and/or device, and it is complete or operable for demonstration. Report should include purpose statement, material list, final plan, results, and conclusion. Student is able to make a presentation and/or answer questions pertaining to the project. |

# INDEX

*Page numbers in **boldface** type refer to figures or tables.*

# INDEX

## M

# INDEX

# INDEX